Lent 2018

To Dona and Sharon ~

With great thanks
to God for your ministry.

Your sister in Christ ~

Julia Faith Parker

My So-Called Biblical Life

My So-Called Biblical Life

Imagined Stories from the World's Best-Selling Book

Julie Faith Parker, *editor*

Foreword by Mark Allan Powell

WIPF & STOCK · Eugene, Oregon

MY SO-CALLED BIBLICAL LIFE
Imagined Stories from the World's Best-Selling Book

Wipf & Stock
An Imprint of Wipf and Stock Publishers
199 W. 8th Ave., Suite 3
Eugene, OR 97401

www.wipfandstock.com

PAPERBACK ISBN: 978-1-4982-3844-1
HARDCOVER ISBN: 978-1-4982-3846-5
EBOOK ISBN: 978-1-4982-3845-8

Manufactured in the U.S.A.   MAY 9, 2017

To all of my students

and especially to New York Theological Seminary's

Class of 2014 Master of Professional Studies Graduates:

Aundray, Lawrence, Eric, Pascual, Jermaine, Kenyatta, Eric,

Max, Manny, Ainsley, James, Kevin, and Naquan;

with deep gratitude for all that you have taught me.

Contents

Contributors

Aundray Jermaine Archer is incarcerated for a murder he maintains he did not commit, although he does admit to a dangerous past. In spite of, or because of, these circumstances, Jermaine decided to become the best person possible by focusing on his passions: languages, education, and the youth. Today, he speaks and writes Spanish and French. While in prison, Jermaine earned a Bachelor of Behavioral Science from Mercy College and a Master of Professional Studies from New York Theological Seminary. He also serves as an advisor to youth assistance programs. Jermaine is most proud of his status as a good son, husband, brother, uncle, father, and stepfather.

Lawrence Bartley holds a Master of Professional Studies from New York Theological Seminary, and a Bachelor of Science from Mercy College via the Hudson Link program. A leader who works on community enhancement legislation and anti-gun violence projects, Lawrence also instructs classes concerning HIV/AIDS and tutors for high school equivalency and college placement exams. Lawrence enjoys acting and directing. He has performed the role of the Scarecrow in *The Wizard of Oz*, as well as assisting in directing a production of Shakespeare's *Twelfth Night*. Most importantly, Lawrence is a husband and father of three.

Evan Cameron is a graduate of Wittenberg University (B.A.) and a current student at Trinity Lutheran Seminary (M. Div.). A native of northeast Ohio, Evan currently lives in Des Moines, Iowa while doing a two year internship at St. Stephen Lutheran Church. He is extremely grateful for his wife Katharine, his family (Jeff, Toni, Eric, Katie, and Ellen), and the many professors and teachers who encouraged him to find and trust his voice. Evan seeks to find beauty and hope in a world that often aims to preach consumerism or despair. He finds this beauty/hope in the national parks, in wonderful and diverse human narratives, in baseball stadiums, in Whitman poetry, and in the grace of Jesus.

Sarah Condon is an ordained Episcopal priest living in Houston, Texas. She is a mother, wife, pastor, and writer. Sarah graduated from Yale Divinity School in 2013 and has served in hospital chaplaincy and parish ministry. Currently, she is an Assistant for Pastoral Care at St. Martin's Episcopal Church and a staff writer for Mockingbird Ministries. As a native Mississippian, Sarah loves a good story. Being a contributor to this project is a real joy for her.

Joseph A. Ebert lives in upstate New York with his wife, Emily, and their dog. He holds a bachelor's degree in architecture, a Master of Architectural Studies in Criticism and Theory from Ohio State University, and an M.A. in Architecture from UCLA's Critical Studies program. Joe is a designer and cultural critic. Currently, he is working on his first book while pursuing independent research. The goal of his writing is to make architectural discourse more accessible to the general public. He is—generally—an optimist.

Clara Garnier-Amouroux is a French student working toward a master's degree in journalism at the *École de Journalisme de Sciences Politiques* in Paris. She earned a bachelor's and master's degree at the *École Normale Supérieure* in Lyon. For the 2014-15 academic year, Clara taught as a French language assistant at Colby College. Clara hopes to produce documentaries about people working to save the planet. She enjoys watching short films on the Sundance website, reading the last page of long novels, and swimming in empty open pools during the winter.

Kenyatta Hughes is a composer, lyricist, actor, and activist. He holds a Master of Professional Studies from New York Theological Seminary. He is active in various organizations including Musical Connections with Carnegie Hall, Rehabilitation through the Arts at Sing Sing Correctional Facility, and Voices from Within, an education initiative that uniquely addresses the epidemic of gun violence directly through the voices of inmates living with the consequences of their choices. A presenter in TEDx Sing Sing, Kenyatta offers the TEDx Talk, "Connecting through Art," which focuses on music and its ability to help people to connect at the purest level.

Emily Phillips Lloyd is an ordained Episcopal priest currently serving as Associate Rector at the Church of Saint Luke in the Fields in New York City. In addition to pastoral duties, she supports a variety of outreach programs and works as chaplain at St. Luke's School. Emily attended the University of North Carolina, Chapel Hill, where she studied Religion, English, and Drama. She earned an M.Div. at Yale Divinity School and a Diploma in Anglican Studies from Berkeley Divinity School. Emily lives on the Lower East Side with her husband, Steve, and their baby, William.

William H. Mohr, J.D., works and lives in New York City balancing global data protection law for a financial firm with lay ministry and spiritual direction in the Brooklyn-Queens Roman Catholic Diocese. With the support of his spouse and two daughters, Bill completed his M.A. at Fordham University in Spirituality and Spiritual Direction in 2014. He has developed a ministry of group spiritual direction in Queens parishes based on Ignatian spirituality. His goals are to complete an accessible edition of select spiritual poetry and to aid those seeking to transcend the experience of our world as a spiritual desert.

Julie Faith Parker is Assistant Professor of Old Testament at Trinity Lutheran Seminary in Columbus, Ohio. She holds a B.A. from Hamilton College, an M.Div. from Union Theological Seminary in New York City, an S.T.M. from Yale Divinity School, and a Ph.D. in Old Testament/Hebrew Bible from Yale University. She is an ordained minister in the United Methodist Church and the author of five books and numerous articles. Julie enjoys singing and running (and ran the NYC Marathon twice). She and her husband, Bill Crawford, have two terrific grown children, Graham and Mari.

Richard P. Poirier is a physician. He graduated from Colby College (Waterville, Maine) in 2012 with a major in Neuroscience and a minor in Religious Studies, then went on to attend medical school at Des Moines University. He is currently working at the Internal Medicine training program at Madigan Army Medical Center in Tacoma, WA as a commissioned captain in the United States Army Medical Corps. A native of central Wisconsin and a college varsity football player, Rich is an avid fan of the Green Bay Packers. He also enjoys kayaking and biking. Studying comparative religions is one of Rich's passions and he is proud to be included in this book.

Emily Sher is a medical student at the School of Osteopathic Medicine Arizona program of A. T. Still University (Mesa, Arizona), where she is studying to become a pediatrician. She graduated from Colby College in 2013 with a major in Religious Studies and a minor in Chemistry. Between college and medical school, she taught chemistry and religious studies at Delbarton High School in Morristown, New Jersey for two years. Over the summers, Emily works to improve the health of low income communities. In her spare time she loves to read, hike, and play with her amazing doodle Rory.

Foreword

Mark Allan Powell

I HEARD A NEW biblical story in Cuba last month.

Jesus was friends with two women named Mary and Martha and they had a brother named Lazarus. The women lived in a nice house in Bethany but their brother was a poor beggar who lay outside the home of a rich man named Dives, where dogs came every day to lick his sores. One day both Lazarus and Dives died and were carried to their eternal homes. Dives went to suffer in hell while Lazarus entered heaven and met the patriarch Abraham. Dives begged Abraham to send Lazarus back to earth to warn his brothers not to do as he had done but Abraham refused, saying that those who do not heed Moses and the prophets will not be convinced even if someone rises from the dead. But then Jesus, who had come to Bethany to comfort his friends in their sorrow, said "I will raise him anyway," and so Lazarus was returned to life.

This is a biblical story not because it is found anywhere in the Bible, but because it is inspired by the Bible. Specifically, it is inspired by a parable that Jesus tells in Luke 16:19–31 and by a miracle story recounted in John 11:1–44. Basically, two separate stories by two different authors have been smushed together to create one new story. The original stories were about two completely different people named Lazarus, one a historical figure and the other a fictitious character in a parable.

Our culture knows stories like this. The supposedly biblical tale of Mary Magdalene, the repentant prostitute who became a follower of Jesus, is found nowhere in scripture; it probably derives from a forced marriage of Luke 7:36–50 with John 20:1–18 so that the "woman of the city" in the first narrative might receive a name and her story might find more satisfactory closure. And every year at Christmas we celebrate the gathering of wise men, shepherds and angels around a manger—a scene that requires collation of Luke 2:1–20 with Matthew 2:1–12.

I used to regard such stories either with amusement (when the audience did not have any way of "knowing better") or with annoyance (when it did). They don't bother me anymore and I doubt that this has anything to do with becoming more open-minded in old age (not a typical process). I think I just understand stories better. It is a matter of understanding how stories work or, to be more precise, it is a matter of understanding how stories *mean*.

We talk a lot about *meaning* and Bible stories. We ask, "What does this story mean?" and we usually assume that there are more-or-less correct answers to that question and more-or-less incorrect answers. I still think that's true, but with some caveats.

First, I have found that people who are concerned with determining the meaning of stories usually conceive of *meaning* as *message*. The meaning of a story can be described in essentially cognitive terms: What is the point of the story? What is the moral of the tale? What do we learn from this story? What messages does it intend to convey?

I like messages (quite a lot) but it is also possible to construe *meaning* as *effect*. Then, the meaning of a story can be described in affective terms: What impact does this story have? How does it make people feel? What does it do to people? Or, simply, what happens when this story is told?

Stories are highly effective media for conveying meaning as effect; they are actually less effective media for conveying meaning as message, if that's all one wants to do.

Let us take a biblical example. One time Jesus wanted to tell his disciples that they should pray always and not lose heart. He could have just told them that, but he didn't. He told them a story: "In a certain city there was a judge who neither feared God nor had respect for people. In that city there was a widow who kept coming to him and saying, 'Grant me justice against my opponent.' For a while he refused; but later he said to himself, 'Though I have no fear of God and no respect for anyone, yet because this widow keeps bothering me, I will grant her justice, so that she may not wear me out by continually coming'" (Luke 18:2–5, NRSV).

Luke 18:1 tells us that Jesus told this story in order to make a point (pray always and don't lose heart). But I submit that if that was *all* he wanted to do, it would have been better to have just said that outright, and then maybe list two or three reasons to support his contention. But no. He told a story that does not just make that point; it is a story that affects people in all sorts of different ways, a story that raises all kinds of questions (Why is God portrayed as an unrighteous judge? Is God reluctant to help us? Is Jesus being ironic? Is he mocking us for thinking of God this way? Why does he depict petitioners as a poor widow? Is that supposed to be humbling? Is he critiquing our assumptions about the marginalized?). The mere fact that the story evokes such questions without answering them indicates that it means something more than just the point it was intended to illustrate. Its capacity to evoke questions is part of its meaning.

I offer this as a caveat to the assumption that there are more-or-less correct answers to the question, "What does this story mean?" Construing meaning as effect rather than message does not require us to abandon that premise altogether. We may still want to consider what effects a story is intended to have, how it is supposed to impact people, what is expected to happen when it is told. But when we leave the cognitive realm for the affective, such categories as "correct" and "incorrect" do become more fluid.

And I have a second caveat. Stories always contain gaps. The word *gaps* is actually a technical term employed by literary critics who have studied polyvalence and the phenomenon of reception. Put simply, the question is, Why do stories inevitably mean different things to different people? And one answer is, stories always contain gaps: ambiguous words, missing details, alternative perspectives and other matters that even careful readers might construe in different ways. Diverse readers inevitably fill those gaps differently, in ways that allow the story to impact them in the ways that they find meaningful.

Gaps can be intentional. Gifted storytellers know that leaving some things unsaid makes a story more effective. So in the famous parable of the Prodigal Son (Luke 15:11–32), Jesus ends the story without telling us how the older brother responds to the impassioned plea of his father to celebrate his brother's return. It is virtually impossible for people to hear this story without asking themselves, "What would I do if I were he?" The story works as well as it does because multiple responses could be defensible.

At other times, the gaps may not be intentional; they are just intrinsic to storytelling. Authors never give us all the information and we are left to speculate on or imagine whatever is not spelled out: What injustice was the widow facing? Did she have a legitimate case? Would her opponent also have had a case worth hearing? What exactly did the judge do for her in the end? How would her opponent have felt about that decision being reached for the reason it had been?

There's more. Readers organize and prioritize the data that stories provide and make meaning from those raw materials. To illustrate this, I will cite a study I did in three different countries on the aforementioned parable of the Prodigal Son. I asked readers a simple question: "Why does the younger brother end up starving in a pig pen?" In the United States, almost everyone responded, "Because he squandered his money living recklessly." But in St. Petersburg, Russia, where more than 600,000 people starved to death in the 1940s, the great majority of respondents said, "Because there was a famine." And in Tanzania, a country that places an extraordinarily high premium on the social value of hospitality, more than 80% answered, "Because no one gave him anything to eat."

So who got the question right? As it turns out, one group did not read the Bible more carefully than the others. Luke's Gospel actually mentions all three reasons for the boy's distress: "He squandered his property in dissolute living. When he had spent everything, a severe famine took place throughout that country and he began to be in need. So he went and hired himself out to one of the citizens of that country, who sent him to his fields to feed the pigs. He would gladly have filled himself with the pods that the pigs were eating; and no one gave him anything" (Luke 15:13b–16). The "gap" in this case is simply one of priorities—virtually all readers in all three countries assumed one reason was the main cause of the boy's trouble while the others were simply aggravating circumstances. But they differed remarkably in identifying the prime culprit.

That's how stories work. That is how they mean. Of all types of literature, stories may be the most generative. Any good story gives birth to more stories. I began this Foreword with examples of forced marriages, instances in which two biblical stories have been brought together in a manner that was probably never intended. But they did reproduce and their offspring have continued to make meaning for millions. It is hard to imagine a crèche without the wise men, and Magdalena the repentant prostitute does get the spotlight song in *Jesus Christ Superstar* ("I Don't Know How to Love Him").

As for the Cuban Lazarus, I heard that story in a house where there was an altar erected to him. On top of the altar, there was a wooden St. Lazarus, covered with sores but surrounded by candles. On the wall there was a painting that showed Jesus welcoming his friend out of the tomb, while in the bottom corner Dives burns in torment and in the top Abraham laments having the man snatched from his bosom after he had forbade his departure.

There is enough traditional Bible scholar in me to still find some of this ridiculous ("They were two different people!"). But the Lazarus devotee found meaning in the hybrid story that would not have arisen from either of the independent ones. One question it evokes is: Why would Jesus return Lazarus to life when Abraham refused to do so? My host had thought much about this and he had come up with an answer: "The tears of women touch the heart of God more deeply than pleas of the damned."

I don't know what to think of this, but the list of things of which I do not know what to think is long (and getting longer). I am just reporting: that's what the biblical story (albeit a story not found in the Bible) means to one Cuban man.

You and I are indebted now to Julie Faith Parker and her students for helping us appreciate the generative power of stories more deeply than ever before. These Bible readers have done their homework. They work closely from the biblical texts; they are attentive to historical context and literary rhetoric. And then, as competent, well-informed readers, they look for the gaps. They discover crevices or windows that invite speculation and then they employ something that has not always been encouraged in academic study: imagination.

In most cases, I think the new stories are ones in keeping with authorial intent, broadly understood. By that I mean that the authors of these stories intended people to read them with imagination and to make meaning from them that those authors might never have come up with on their own. Storytellers usually want their stories to have meaning that the teller did not anticipate—and if not, well then they shouldn't be telling stories, because that's what stories do. That is how they mean.

Mark Allan Powell is the Robert and Phyllis Leatherman Professor of New Testament at Trinity Lutheran Seminary in Columbus, Ohio. An internationally renowned Bible scholar, he has authored or edited over thirty books, including *Introducing the New Testament*, *Loving Jesus*, and the *HarperCollins Bible Dictionary*.

Acknowledgments

WORKING ON THIS BOOK has been a joy; the most exciting part has been helping my students evolve from writers into authors. I would like to thank all of my students who inspire me daily and give my work meaning.

I am grateful to those who helped bring this book to its published form. At Wipf and Stock, Brian Palmer and Ben Dieter offered support, guidance, and understanding. Leslie Thayer Piper, the copyeditor, has been my cherished friend for decades; she is truly a talented editor. Leslie's careful attention to this manuscript has been a great gift to this book and to me.

I am blessed with wonderful colleagues. My fellow faculty and the administration at Trinity Lutheran Seminary have been supportive throughout this project. Dr. Mark Allan Powell graciously agreed to write the Foreword, providing an essay from an internationally renowned biblical scholar alongside writings of new authors. I am also deeply grateful to John Collins, Serene Jones, and Phyllis Trible for endorsing this book.

Finally, I would like to thank my family. My husband, Bill Crawford, and our grown children, Graham and Mari, encourage me in my work and love me all the time. What could be greater than that?

Abbreviations

ABD—*The Anchor Bible Dictionary on CD-ROM.* Logos Library System Version 2.1. 1997. Print ed.: Edited by David Noel Freedman. 6 vols. New York: Doubleday, 1992.

ASV—American Standard Version (1901)

BCE—Before Common Era. A non-confessional way of referring to the time before the birth of Jesus (in lieu of BC [before Christ]).

CE—Common Era. A non-confessional way of referring to the time after the birth of Jesus (in lieu of AD [anno Domini]).

DDD—*The Dictionary of Deities and Demons in the Bible.* Edited by Karel van der Toorn, Bob Becking, and Pieter W. Van der Horst. 2nd ed. Leiden: Brill, 1999.

HALOT—Koehler, Ludwig and Walter Baumgartner. *The Hebrew and Aramaic Lexicon of the Old Testament, Study Edition,* rev. ed. Walter Baumgartner and Johann J. Stamm. Translated and edited under the supervision of M. E. J. Richardson. 2 vols. Leiden: Brill, 2001.

JAMA—*Journal of the American Medical Association*

JBL—*Journal of Biblical Literature*

JSOT—*Journal for the Study of the Old Testament*

KJV—King James Version (1611)

NAS—New American Standard (1977)

NJB—New Jerusalem Bible (1985)

NJPS—*Tanakh: The Holy Scriptures: The New JPS Translation according to the Traditional Hebrew Text* (1985).

NKJV—New King James Version (1982)

NRSV—New Revised Standard Version (1989)

RSV—Revised Standard Version (1952)

Introduction

ONE OF MY FAVORITE paintings is Henri Matisse's *The Dance*. Perhaps you know it—five graceful orange figures form a circle against a simple and striking background of cobalt blue and emerald green. The dancers are all holding hands, except for a slight break in the circle between the figures on the left side of the painting. This small opening between two hands is the artist's invitation to the viewer, who is invited to enter into the circle. This book is like that space, beckoning you to join in the dance of the Bible's swirling stories.

Dancing is an apt analogy for reading the Bible. Like entering a dance that has already begun, we just jump in and start to read. The words move us and may even change our mood. Yet, like a sophisticated tango, the Bible is complicated. A bit like stepping *slow slow quick-quick slow* with alternating feet, people often find reading the Bible overwhelming. They may feel awkward, uncomfortable, or confused. They may stay on the sidelines and feel left out, reading the Bible a little, or dropping away entirely. Many readers then miss out on experiencing the world's best-selling book and arguably the world's greatest literary treasure. But who can blame them?

The Bible does not come with a step-by-step manual and has no concern for teaching us how to approach it. A student of mine, who had extensive knowledge of classical texts, once remarked, "These stories are so sparse . . . perhaps because they come from the desert." I wanted to defend the text's riches, but I couldn't disagree. Biblical narratives are unapologetically cryptic; the reader often has to work to envision what is going on. Rarely does the text deign to supply even simple adjectives. What did Moses look like? Or Jesus? We're never told. Characters' motives remain secret. Why does Noah believe God and build the ark? Why does Mary listen to Gabriel then willingly agree to bear a child? No one knows. Sometimes critical information is simply missing. How did Eve realize that she should not eat the forbidden fruit since she hadn't been created when God gave this instruction? Why does Abraham agree to sacrifice his long-awaited son? We can only surmise.

Yet this mysterious quality that makes the Bible confounding also makes it intriguing. Readers need to get involved to appreciate or even understand this text—and they do. Ancient rabbis would answer the Bible's open questions and write down their answers, creating a literary art form called *midrash* (from the Hebrew word *dārash* meaning "to seek" or "to enquire"). While these learned men were held in such high respect that their writings have been treasured for centuries, anyone can engage the text to make it become more alive in their imagination. When we pause to envision a situation in the text, the human emotions and struggles that simmer beneath the surface emerge. When we explore unanswered questions and provide missing details, faded ancient words become infused with living color.

The contributors to *My So-Called Biblical Life* imbue the text with life and energy, almost like a dance. The essays in this book have been selected from many that I have read over the years from my students at Yale University (New Haven, Conn.), Fordham University (Bronx, NY), Colby College (Waterville, Maine), Trinity Lutheran Seminary (Columbus, Ohio), and New York Theological Seminary with a program in Sing Sing Maximum Security Prison (Ossining, NY). As relayed in the contributor biographies, these authors come from diverse backgrounds and now fulfill a range of vocations: doctor, actor, priest, musician/composer, professor, activist, journalist, seminarian, lawyer, chaplain, medical student, community organizer, architect, youth advisor, and parent. Some are still in school and some are still behind bars. Their personalities and experiences subtly contribute to the variety, depth, and nuance of the stories in this book.

My own role in the creation of this book has exceeded that of a typical editor. I have revised and written sections of some essays to enhance the drama of the narrative and to keep the story consistent with knowledge of the biblical world. I am grateful for my students' trust in this process.

Each essay is based on a specific passage from either the Hebrew Bible (or Old Testament) or the New Testament, which appears in an original translation. I have translated these Hebrew and Greek texts adhering closely to the biblical languages to give the reader a clear sense of the ancient texts. These passages also help the reader avoid the trap of confusing the story of the Bible with the fictitious essay. The writer of each essay works from and adds to the biblical passage but never contradicts what is already in the Bible. The imagined stories dovetail with the original translations.

Further resources help the reader engage with the essays. Footnotes explain about the language in the text or the world of the Bible. Following each story, three discussion questions invite readers to connect with the story and reflect on how the imagined narrative expands their understanding of the biblical text. The bibliography at the end of the chapter provides resources for readers to delve more deeply into the material.

The arrangement of the essays follows the canonical order of the selected texts in the Bible. Just as most of the Christian Bible is the Old Testament, the majority of these stories are based on the Hebrew Bible. Four writers address the New Testament; like the four Gospel writers, they offer different perspectives on the life of Jesus. Twelve chapters in total recall the emphasis on twelve in the Bible: twelve tribes of Israel in the Old Testament and twelve disciples in the New Testament. *My So-Called Biblical Life* offers tribute to the Bible in its re-imagining of the text and also in its structure.

The first story by Aundray Jermaine Archer is unusual in this collection as Archer gives voice to the serpent in the Garden of Eden (Gen 3). Whereas the other essays are bound by practical constraints of life in biblical times, "Not Sneaky but Smart: Sagacity from the Speaking Snake" dwells in the land of myth where all things are possible, even snakes who like to chat. The serpent here bears no relationship to the devil. Rather, this intelligent reptilian narrator uses persuasive reasoning, clear logic, and textual insights to challenge commonly-held assumptions about Adam, and especially Eve. The story of Adam and Eve may be the best-known tale in the entire Bible, but it has never before been known like this.

Leah is the matriarch of Jewish lineage about whom little is known. In the Bible she speaks a few times, mostly to pronounce the birth of her sons (see Gen 29:16—30:21). The older daughter of Laban, and sister to the prettier Rachel, Leah is switched for her sister on the night that Rachel and Jacob are to wed (Gen 29:17–24). Jacob thinks he has slept with Rachel, only to discover in the morning that he has been tricked. The Bible tells us how he feels as he expresses his shock, hurt, and outrage to Laban (Gen 29:25). But how did Leah feel? What was her response to the terrible position in which her father placed her? The Bible provides no insights as to how Leah views her experience as a pawn in a man's game; Clara Garnier-Amouroux steps into this silence. Her essay's title, "What About Me?" has Leah pose a question that Bible writers do not let women ask.

In "Just Before the Abyss: The Legacy of Korah," Joseph Ebert takes two texts from the book of Numbers and weaves them together in a cause-and-effect scenario (Numbers 15:32–36; 16:1–33). While readers of the Bible tend to view Moses as a caring leader bringing his people from slavery to liberation, Ebert's narrative suggests that Moses acts more like a tyrannical warlord or Taliban chief. Moses' primary motivation for the laws that he upholds seem to be safeguarding his own power, and that of his brother Aaron, with little regard for human life. Korah, the protagonist in Numbers 16, emerges as the hero of this narrative. Yet in the story, as in the Bible, this hero is unable to save anyone, including himself.

"Only Hope" by Sarah Condon is a prequel to Judges 19. This essay visits the episode of the Levite's concubine from the perspective of the concubine's mother. The Bible provides no reference to the character who is narrator for Condon's tale. Accordingly, the story hints that the concubine's mother may have died from illness before the incident relayed in Judges. Through her essay, Condon invites readers to consider the concubine as a teenage girl with a name, skills, hopes, and a family who loved her. This fleshed out understanding of the Levite's concubine magnifies the tragedy of her brutal end.

Emily Phillips Lloyd's story, "The Outing," is both traditional and feminist in its approach to the text. Phillips Lloyd gives the name Tashere to Pharaoh's daughter and King Solomon's wife (see 1 Kgs 3:1). The essay is based on 1 Kgs 3:16–28, a well-known tale about two women who come before the king both claiming to be the mother of the same baby boy. Tashere narrates this incident, subtly revealing her profound influence on her wise husband. On one hand, this Egyptian princess is an adoring and agreeable spouse; on the other, she is clear about her power and how to use it.

My own contribution, "Vessels of Hope," appears in the order of biblical sequence, but was the last story added to this book. While working with my students' essays, I felt increasingly compelled to write my own. I chose the story of Elisha and the Debt Collateral Children (2 Kings 4:1–7) because so few people know this short, gripping miracle tale. I also wanted to question the common assumption that women in the Bible only care about having sons. This story portrays a biblical world that affords women far more agency than we usually imagine.

"Appeasing the Death-Loving God" by Richard Poirier points to a practice in the Bible that will surprise many readers: child sacrifice. While scholars debate whether or not ancient Israelites sacrificed their children as an offering, numerous biblical texts attest to ritual killing of children to appease a deity. Poirier's story uses two verses in Jeremiah (7:31; 32:35) as a starting place for imagining a family faced with gut-rending decisions in the face of drought. Through the eyes of a boy, the reader sees how and why awful choices must be made . . . and the hope that they offer while bringing despair.

Emily Sher's essay, "He Didn't Name *Me*: I am Gomer" weaves a story around the character of Gomer, wife of the prophet Hosea (Hosea 1:2–6, 8–9; 2:2–10). This narrative was born from the writer's frustration with the lack of information that she could find on Gomer while writing a research paper for class. Sher decided to create the tale of Gomer's life, as she imagined it. This story combines romance and violence, giving Gomer the voice that the text denies her. I find Sher's tale so moving that I have read it out loud in classes on Hosea. By the end, I am nearly in tears.

The first essay on the New Testament is "The Rich Young Ruler" by William Mohr, based on the account of a wealthy man who questions Jesus about how to inherit eternal life (Mark 10:17–22). In Mohr's narrative, the protagonist is a Roman ruler who explains his curiosity about Jesus and follows reports of his ministry, death, and resurrection, leading him to the scene of the Pentecost (Acts 2). This powerful man's initial refusal to join with Jesus changes over time, but only as the requirements to become a follower of Jesus shift as well. This essay invites readers to ponder the sacrifices that faith can demand, and why we so often refuse to make them.

Evan Cameron continues a focus on Jesus in the Gospel of Mark with his graphic story of Jesus' crucifixion (Mark 15:16–39). Even Christians who are very familiar with the story of Jesus on the cross rarely envision the cruel and gruesome scenario with such painful and precise detail. "Revelation" reports the events of Jesus' torture and death through the eyes of the Roman centurion who oversees the crucifixion with unwavering justification of his actions—then changes at the bitter end.

Lawrence Bartley imagines one of the Bible's best-known stories in his retelling of the parable of the Good Samaritan (Luke 10:25–37). The hero of this account is not driven purely by compassion to help the wounded traveler on the side of the road. Rather, a complex mix of motivations inspires him to act, then later question what he has done. Seeking clarity, the Samaritan asks Jesus to help him understand the ramifications of these deeds. As he eventually realizes the extent of Jesus' power, the Samaritan answers his own question: "How Could He Know?"

The final story, "Fisherman," focuses on Jesus after his resurrection. Based on John 21:1–24, this story is told by an anonymous friend of Peter's who fishes with the disciples. A long fruitless night becomes an eventful fish-filled morning when the risen Jesus appears on the beach. This honest and compelling story raises hard questions about the risks of discipleship and the cost of faith.

Together, these twelve essays create a book well-suited for use in a wide range of contexts, in addition to personal reading. *My So-Called Biblical Life* can provide supplementary reading for courses on the Bible, in high school, undergraduate, or graduate classrooms. Congregations will find this book a helpful resource for teaching about the Bible. A church or synagogue Bible study could easily be organized around its contents, for either large or small group reflection. This book could be used on religious retreats or with confirmation classes. Each story takes fifteen to twenty minutes to read out loud. In many religious traditions, the preacher could expressively read an essay as the sermon in a worship service. This book offers further possibilities for programs. A designated leader might present a story or two through a dramatic reading, followed by discussion. More ambitiously, the stories could be staged by actors as a series of monologues. Book groups, outside of a religious or educational context, will also find the stories and subsequent questions engaging. Through any or all of these venues, *My So-Called Biblical Life* invites the reader to a fresh way of experiencing the literary treasure that is the world's best-selling book.

Like a dance, this book is also about action. Three of the contributors to this book are in prison and half of the royalties are donated to the Exodus Transitional Community (www.etcny.org), which helps people after incarceration. Like the freed Israelites who wandered in the desert for forty years, people released from prison find themselves in a modern wilderness, trying to survive and thrive in a challenging environment. Located in East Harlem, New York, Exodus offers support services and job training that help to break the cycle of recidivism. Thank you for your role in contributing to this life-changing program through this book.

While offering educational and transformative benefits, this book seeks to be enjoyable. Like dancing, reading this book may be surprisingly emotional. As you move through its pages, you will recognize common struggles and universal hopes that bind people together across thousands of miles and thousands of years. Ultimately, *My So-Called Biblical Life* seeks to honor a core message of the Bible by upholding our shared humanity.

Not Sneaky but Smart

Sagacity from the Speaking Snake

AUNDRAY JERMAINE ARCHER

1 Now the serpent was more crafty than any other creature of the field that the LORD God had made. So he said to the woman, "Did God really say that you should not eat from any tree in the garden?"[1] *2* The woman said to the serpent, "We can eat of the fruit of the trees in the garden; *3* but from the fruit of the tree that is in the midst of the garden, God said, 'You should not eat from it, and you should not touch it, or you will die.'" *4* But the serpent said to the woman, "You surely will not die; *5* for God knows that on the day that you eat of it your eyes will be opened, and you will be like God, knowing good and evil." *6* So when the woman saw that the tree was good for food, and that it was a delight to the eyes, and that the tree was desirable to become wise, she took of its fruit and ate; and she also gave some to her husband with her, and he ate. *7* Then the eyes of both of them were opened, and they knew that they were naked; and they sewed fig leaves together and made loincloths for themselves.

8 They heard the sound of the LORD God walking around in the garden in the wind of the day, and the man and his woman hid themselves from the presence of the LORD God in the midst of the trees of the garden. *9* But the LORD God called to the man, and said to him,

---

1. The serpent addresses both Adam and Eve, as evidenced by the Hebrew plural verb forms for the word "eat" in v. 1 (*tōʾkəlû*), and "die" in v. 4 (*təmutûn*). Eve accordingly answers the serpent with the first person plural in v. 2 ("we can eat"; *nōʾkēl*).

"Where are you?" *10* He said, "I heard your voice in the garden, and I was afraid, because I was naked; and I hid myself." *11* He said, "Who informed you that you were naked? Did you eat from the tree that I commanded you not to eat from?!" *12* The man said, "The woman whom you gave to be with me—she gave me from the tree, and I ate." *13* Then the LORD God said to the woman, "What is this that you have done?" The woman said, "The serpent beguiled me, and I ate." *14* The LORD God said to the serpent, "Because you have done this, cursed are you among all the beasts and among all creatures of the field; upon your belly you shall go, and dust you shall eat all the days of your life."

—GENESIS 3:1–14

I AM HERE TO set the story straight. For countless generations, I have been associated with evil. Yet am I responsible for introducing sin to the world? Am I so malicious? Is that accurate? Is it fair? Let us revisit one of the most infamous moments in the history of humanity. Listen to my side of the story as I present my reasoning to you, for I was there. My realm is the myth where all things are possible—even speaking snakes—and time is transcended. I ask that you maintain an open mind as we journey together through the past and into the present, remembering my conversation in that most famous of gardens.

While my identity is relatively straightforward, there are many false rumors concerning my role in the "Fall of Man," or "Original Sin," as it is often called. I do not appreciate either term; these phrases are inappropriate at best, misleading at worst. Therefore, let us refer to the notorious event in question as the "Eve and Adam Controversy."

Your critical mind must have many unanswered questions after reviewing what transpires in the Garden of Eden, as recorded in the scriptures. I have read these scriptures that so many cherish as sacred—yet so many questions still remain unasked. For instance, since the word "sin" is never used, why do interpreters insist that Eve and Adam sinned? And if they did sin, why, as a result of this sin, did they become "like God, knowing good and evil"?[2] Does this imply that God is sinful, because God knows evil? Does it indicate that it is sinful to know the difference between good

---

2. Gen 3:5.

and evil? Is that not the basis of morality? Before we attend to these questions, let us first review the genesis of the Controversy.

I am not present "in the beginning," but can't you see that prior to humans I was God's special creature? I alone among God's many animals possessed the power of speech. There in the garden I had a brief and widely remembered conversation with Eve. Although the scripture that came later documents me speaking only twice, Eve and I had enjoyed many discussions prior to the day in question. In fact, God and I also spoke quite regularly. While few recognize our relationship since it is not in scripture, God and I had been wonderful conversation partners until God decided to create humans.

With everything you have been taught about me, can you stomach the possibility that *I* am made in God's image? Consider this idea, not in the context of your future existence, but in that of "time before time." Put aside all preconceived notions and focus on what your scriptures say. To whom does God direct the words, "Let us make a human in our image, in our likeness"?[3] Future explanations will allege that the phrase "our image" indicates "Israel's demythologized version of the ancient Near Eastern Pantheon"[4] or is to "avoid the idea of an immediate resemblance of humans to God," or was spoken in a manner of "deliberation."[5] Many scholarly minds have opined that this plural pronoun refers to a heavenly court or a heavenly host that consults with the great supreme God.[6] Some Christian commentators even understand God's plural self-reference as indicating the Holy Trinity: Father, Son, and Holy Ghost.[7] But I ask you, are any of these figures mentioned in this story? Does the text in any way suggest that otherworldly beings of the time before history—much less the figure of Christ who lived much later—are present at all? Clearly not. But there *I* was, there with God in the garden. Refer to Genesis 1:27, in which God creates a human in *his* own image. Why is this relevant? Not to assert that God is male, but rather because it constitutes proof that God can speak in the singular. Therefore, when God speaks in the plural,[8] the words are deliberate

---

3. Gen 1:26.

4. Kselman, "Genesis," 86.

5. Westermann, *Genesis 1–11*, 144–45.

6. Davidson, *Genesis 1–11*, 24.

7. Ibid.

8. Gen 1:26.

and directed at another being: namely me. God and I are discussing making a human in *our* image; ergo, God and I share an image.

You may counter this notion and refer me to the second creation story.[9] In Genesis 2:7, God forms Adam out of the dust of the ground and breathes life into this earth creature. In Genesis 2:16–17, Adam is firmly instructed—even threatened—not to eat of the tree of the knowledge of good and evil. The punishment is immediate death. Softening a bit, God then decides that Adam should not be alone and decides to form more creatures from the ground, as God had created him. God then orders these animals to parade in front of Adam so that he might choose a mate. As the special speaking creature, I do not march in that parade but I find it entertaining to watch Adam refuse one animal after another. If Adam had chosen an eagle or a tortoise or a giraffe as a companion, what would have become of humanity? But since none of these animals were suitable (good thing for you), God made Eve. Adam was thrilled with this new creature and exclaimed a profound affirmation of their equality: "This at last is bone of my bone and flesh of my flesh!"[10] However, I later came to discover that Eve was clearly the brains of this couple.

Adam and his mate, Eve, were then in the garden, along with me, many other creatures, and the forbidden fruits. I had frequently feasted on these now-legendary fruits long before the Eve and Adam Controversy. Why was I not punished then, you ask? I *was* punished—by God's creation of humans. Prior to them, I was God's favored creature as the only animal who spoke. Upon their creation, they became the final achievement, the mark of "genius" (or so it was thought).

No doubt you are questioning my motivations as I share with you my unique state of privilege with God. What are my intentions? Your scriptures say that I was "more crafty than any other creature of the field."[11] I ask you: is "crafty" synonymous with "evil"? *Pas de tout.* "Crafty" implies cleverness and the ability to use knowledge. In other places where this word occurs in your scripture, it is a compliment for someone who is intelligent![12] I

9. In the first creation story (Gen 1:1—2:4a), God speaks the world into being and pronounces it good. The second creation story (Gen 2:4b—3:24), held by scholars to be from a separate and earlier source, tells the story of Adam and Eve.

10. Gen 2:23a.

11. Gen 3:1.

12. The Hebrew word (*ārûm*) used to describe the serpent in Gen 3:1 can be translated as "crafty," "subtle," "shrewd," "clever," or "prudent," all words expressing purposeful intelligence. (See Prov 12:16, 23; 13:16; 14:8; 22:3; 27:12.) This word for informed

realized that I had fallen from grace in God's eyes, and I was smart enough to detect that Adam and Eve were the result of that falling out. I had every reason to be angry, but I was not. Instead, I was curious; curiosity is one of my core character traits, as is common among strong thinkers.

When God made the heavens, the earth, the birds, the fish, and all animals, "God saw that it was good."[13] But when God formed Eve and Adam, suddenly creation was "very good."[14] I immediately questioned whether they could live up to God's "very good" expectations, yet I harbored no ill will. I did, however, take slight offense at God giving them dominion "over every living thing that moves upon the earth,"[15] because that included me. This presented conflict, as I did not look favorably upon my being dominated by creatures less intelligent than myself, and furthermore, who were created after me. Nevertheless, my actions were based not on jealousy, but on curiosity. I wanted to know what these human creatures would do with their "dominion."

Before the Controversy, I constantly heard from God how very good Adam and Eve were, how the world was perfect now that they existed, how happy God was with them. This remembrance may ring of jealousy, but I beg to differ. The song simply grew stale, especially because I knew that they were not "very good"; they simply did not know good from evil. Ignorance is not the same as inner goodness or pure innocence; it is simply a lack of knowledge. Adam and Eve were no better than I, and given the opportunity, they too became curious and exercised free will. Please note: they did not come to easily dominate me.

Let us review the false interpretations perpetuated by misreading Genesis 3:1–14.

Fallacy Number One: *I introduce evil into the world.* How could this be true? The tree of the knowledge of good and evil existed prior to my creation with the ability to endow with this knowledge those who partook of its fruit. Therefore, I could not create a concept that already existed and was knowable through a tree in God's garden.

---

thinking (*ārûm*) is similar to the word for "naked" (*ʿērōm*), foreshadowing the fate of Adam and Eve once they eat of the fruit. (Both Hebrew words come from the same three consonants: *ayin, resh, mem.*) Adam and Eve will gain awareness (*ārûm*) that they are without clothes (*ʿērōm*); see Gen 3:7, 10, 11.

13. Gen 1:4, 10, 12, 18, 25.

14. Gen 1:31.

15. Gen 1:28.

Fallacy Number Two: *I seduce Eve because Adam is incorruptible.* This lie has been greatly exaggerated. Take out your scriptures and notice that Adam was beside Eve when the deed is done. Genesis 3:6 informs you that after eating the fruit, Eve offered "some to her husband, *who was with her*, and he ate."[16] Adam never even *attempted* to interrupt or cease our encounter. Rather, he sat idly by as she and I discussed the powerful and pleasing fruit. He watched as she took a bite and said *nary one word*. Eve noticed the yearning in his eyes and considerately invited him to share in this scrumptious snack. Adam didn't pause for a second, but ate the fruit, rather voraciously, I might add. He did not say anything to remind Eve of God's threats—threats that she had not even heard directly, because she had not yet been created![17] Do not let the legacy of scathing interpretations mislead you; Adam was a willing participant in this affair.

Fallacy Number Three: *I intentionally caused the downfall of humankind.* You may accept this idea because of how I have been depicted. You may believe that I am the personification of evil or even the devil himself—outrageous! While I am admittedly "crafty," your scriptures do not show me to be "evil" at all! Yes, I informed Eve of the consequences of eating from the Tree of Knowledge before she does so, but I never proposed that she eat. I simply asked her about her conversation with the deity. Then I told her that she would not die if she ate but would become like God. Did she gain knowledge of good and evil after eating the fruit, like God? Yes. Did she die after eating the fruit? No. Did Adam die? Only when he was nine hundred and thirty years old![18] Tell me, how did I lie or cause humanity's downfall?

Fallacy Number Four: *Eve and Adam committed original sin.* Nowhere in the text are their actions described as sinful. If anything, Eve knew the consequences of eating the fruit: she would become like God, knowing good and evil. Ironically, both Adam and Eve were *already* like God because they had been created *in God's image* (only a clever mind like mine can detect such subtleties). Eve demonstrated an additional likeness to God in becoming the first creature to see something as "good." She saw that the fruit of the tree was *good*, even before eating from it.[19] Prior to her realization, only God saw things as good. Eve realized that the tree was "a delight

---

16. See Parker, "Blaming Eve Alone," 731–42.

17. Gen 2:15–17.

18. Gen 5:5.

19. Gen 3:6.

to the eyes, *and also desirable to become wise.*"[20] This constitutes proof that Eve was not rebelling from God or being willfully disobedient; rather, this smart woman was searching for wisdom. I was not instigating a rebellion, but rather sharing in the knowledge that I had already received from eating of the tree. To deem her actions wicked is to assert that learning good from evil is sinful, an idea that knocks knowledge and eschews ethics. Such notions should be rejected by intelligent and moral thinkers.

Fallacy Number Five: *I am a tempter.* I will admit that before our fateful conversation, I knew that Eve would find this fruit compelling. From our previous encounters, I had discovered that she enjoyed learning and was good at naming reasons for her actions; she would not find becoming like God distasteful. Just prior to the Controversy, I had been walking through the garden, minding my own business, when I overheard Eve and Adam talking. I paused, for fear the leaves crunching beneath my feet would betray my presence . . . and I listened. Adam told Eve that they would die if they ate of the exotic delights from the tree of the knowledge of good and evil. I watched Eve eyeing the ripe fruit and I could see that her mind was churning. We were on good terms, so I stepped out from the shadows and asked if God had told them they would die if they ate from it. Eve replied in the affirmative. I was struck by the curiosity and hunger in her eyes—she sought wisdom, and this treasure was obtainable only by experiencing the illicit fruit. I had eaten from this tree and here I was to tell about it. I felt compelled to inform Eve of the truth that she would not die if she sampled the orbs that she so clearly desired. So I honestly explained, "God knows that on the day that you eat of it your eyes will be opened, and you will be like God, knowing good and evil."[21] This may be "crafty" on my part, but please note that I never "tempted" or "seduced" her into eating. I just reliably explained the ramifications of such an act.

After our brief exchange, I could see Eve concentrating on the attractive fruit, deliberating what to do next. She noticed that the tree "was good for food," "a delight to the eyes," and "desirable to become wise."[22] Her delicate fingers caressed the skin of the fruit until she finally plucked one off of the tree, brought it to her face, and inhaled deeply, luxuriating in the alluring aroma. She took a slow, delicious bite, and her eyes danced with joy; I could tell she had somehow gained the knowledge that she craved. Also, she did

20. Gen 3:6.
21. Gen 3:5.
22. Gen 3:6.

not die, as I had informed her. I had spoken the truth! Eve, now enlightened, saw Adam's desire to partake and she shared this delectable experience with him. Adam also enjoyed this fruit, and their pleasure illuminated the garden. Yet once the deed was done, they suddenly realized that they were naked. Although they initially sought to see "good," the first thing they noticed when they became enlightened was their bodies (which by some have been construed as evil). Instead of realizing they were like God, knowing good and evil, they learned that they were not even like each other. In an effort to cover their differences, they began making clothes from fig leaves. Perhaps knowledge of how to do this also came from eating the fruit.

The mood had changed, and I reasoned that I should make my exit. But before I could take one step, I heard God stomping through the garden. I knew God would not be pleased, so I struck a casual pose, fingering the leafy green bushes and whistling with the birds. Eve and Adam, on the other hand, tried to hide . . . from God! How do you hide *from God*? In God's garden, no less? Alas, they had not become as enlightened as I had hoped.

The rest is legendary. God asked how they knew they were naked, and Adam (in becoming the world's first snitch) pointed the finger at Eve. In a shameless effort to deflect blame from himself, Adam even tossed some of it in God's direction by declaring, "The woman whom *you* gave to be with me—*she* gave me from the tree, and I ate."[23] Eve found herself in a compromising situation. On one side, she had Adam, her mate, who expeditiously blamed his behavior on her in the face of God's wrath. I stood on the other side, the one who had told her the truth but remained silent once she was accused. In the middle was God, her angry judge. Intelligent Eve became one woman under duress facing a triumvirate of males.

As it is written, God punished us all. Prior to the creation of humans I strolled the Garden of Eden proudly, my head held high and my back straight as I relished the feeling of the warm soil between my toes. I stood over seven feet tall, and I fondly recall the *thud* of my soles against the ground with every long stride I took. I savored the sweet fruits of the garden, enjoying their citrus perfumes that wafted through the air and pervaded my nostrils. I tasted the smell with my tongue, as scents invited me to their lush, green bushes to pluck their juicy delicacies. Often, the most succulent fruits positioned themselves high up in the trees, leading me to swing from limb to limb in pursuit of them. You ask why I no longer walk with my head high, why I no longer stand seven feet tall, why I no longer

23. Gen 3:12.

possess legs and feet, and why I now eat dust from the ground instead of fruit from the branches? Some call it "etiology";[24] I call it vindictiveness. All I did was tell the truth, but God was in an angry mood once the disobedience occurred. God punished me in other ways too; whereas I once interacted with Adam and Eve regularly, humans are now fearful of me and step on me to kill me. God also penalized Adam and Eve, making Adam toil for food and making Eve suffer pangs in childbirth, among other distresses, including exiling them from the garden.

Once Eve and Adam left the garden, my story in your scripture was over. I could no longer speak, but my intelligence has remained with me so I decided to write my story to provide the true account of what happened.

I did not commit evil as alleged in Genesis. I simply predicted what would happen and my prediction was correct: Eve became wise. God even said to me, "Look: the human one has become like one of us, knowing good and evil."[25] Is this not evidence that I spoke the truth? When has telling the truth been associated with evil? My answer: when the truth poses a threat to the one in power. Contrary to what you've been taught, this is the true lesson of the Eve and Adam Controversy: beware that speaking the truth can lead to demonization.

Instead of laying blame with me, Eve, or Adam for that matter, I assert that God is the One to be looked upon with a wary eye. God had not even warned Adam and Eve of the possible punishments of physical labor or hard pregnancies or banishment from the garden. God told Adam he could "surely eat from any tree in the garden"[26] and directly warned, "but from the tree of the knowledge of good and evil, you must not eat from it—for on the day that you eat from it you will surely die."[27] But Adam and Eve didn't die, so why should they believe God? After the Controversy, God punished all three of us, tossing in human death and burial for good measure.[28] Therefore, God did not speak the entire truth when he warned them not to eat of the fruit, because they were later punished in more ways than previously threatened. Simply put, God changed the rules after they ate the fruit, therefore God acted deceptively, not I.

---

24. An etiology is a story of origins that explains how an observable phenomenon came to be.

25. Gen 3:22.

26. Gen 2:16.

27. Gen 2:17.

28. Gen 3:19.

Furthermore, Adam was like a brand new computer: he had no internal thought processes aside from those with which God programmed him. Adam did not ask questions or think for himself; he simply did as God instructed. Eve, on the other hand, was what you might call the "upgrade." She represented the newer, advanced model. If you create something, then make a later model, the subsequent model stands a good chance of outperforming the old model. (If this were not the case, Apple would have stopped after the first iPhone.) Adam did not possess Eve's critical mind; he accepted God's threats as fact. Like me, Eve had a curious mind, which is why we were friends and conversation partners. No one, not even God, could tell her something and expect her to accept it at face value. The day before Eve ate of the fruit, I asked her why God gave her such a beautiful mind if she was forbidden from exercising it. She mused over my question but could not come up with a convincing answer.

Eve was so smart that it was only a matter of time before she realized she could become like God. She wanted to gain knowledge, unlike Adam who preferred to be led. When God told Adam to not eat the fruit, Adam did as told. Later, when Eve offered Adam the fruit, he took it *with no resistance*. As a born follower, he asked no questions. Eve, on the other hand, was a born leader. She was special, the first creature to know good when she saw it, and she demonstrated to me that I was not strange because I too was a thinking, curious creature. There is nothing sinful in simply asking questions. Through Eve I could prove to God that these chosen human creatures were, in essence, no different from me. Under the right circumstances, they too would act out their curiosity—Eve as the leader and Adam as the follower.

Now you know my side of the story. Go back and look at Genesis 3:1–14. Yes, that account of the Controversy leaves out some of the details I have provided for you, but no information that I have offered here contradicts your sacred text. Instead of bringing Eve and Adam to sin, I helped them gain knowledge.

The choice is yours. You can be like Adam and accept without question the things you have been told. Or you can be like Eve and ponder and investigate to ascertain your own truth. The record of the Controversy shows that I spoke honestly, whereas God did not.

Did I introduce sin to the world? Am I evil? Has my reasoning persuaded you?

Consider carefully my insights and tell me, please: Who do you say I am?

Discussion Questions

1. This story portrays Eve as an intelligent leader and Adam as a passive follower. Do you think that this interpretation of Genesis 3 can be sustained by the biblical text? Why or why not?

2. The snake here tries to convince you that he is not evil, contrary to popular opinion and many interpretations that associate the serpent with the devil. Are you persuaded by the snake's point that he is more curious and crafty than malicious and malevolent?

3. Eve desires knowledge of good and evil. If you could have instant knowledge about one thing, what would it be?

Bibliography

Davidson, Robert. *Genesis 1–11*. Cambridge Bible Commentary. Cambridge: Cambridge University Press, 1973.

Kselman, Jon S. "Genesis." In *HarperCollins Bible Commentary*, edited by James L. Mays, et al., 83–118. New York: HarperCollins, 2000.

Parker, Julie Faith. "Blaming Eve Alone: Translation, Omission, and Implications of עמה in Genesis 3:6b." *JBL* 132.4 (2013) 729–47.

Westermann, Claus. *Genesis 1–11: A Commentary*. Translated by John J. Scullion. Minneapolis: Fortress, 1984.

What about Me?

The Tale of the Forgotten Sister

Clara Garnier-Amouroux

1 Jacob got on his feet, and went to the land of the Easterners. *2* He looked and there was a well in the field! Three flocks of sheep were lying there beside it, because the flocks were watered from that well. The stone on the opening of the well was large. *3* When all the flocks were gathered there, they would roll the stone from the mouth of the well and water the sheep, then put the stone back on the opening of the well in its place.

4 Jacob said to them, "My brothers, where are you from?" They said, "We are from Haran." *5* He said to them, "Do you know Laban son of Nahor?" They said, "We know him." *6* He said to them, "Is it well with him?" "Yes," they said, "and here is his daughter Rachel, coming with the sheep." *7* He said, "It is still midday; it is not time for the animals to be gathered together. Water the sheep, and go, pasture them." *8* But they said, "We cannot until all the flocks are gathered together, and the stone is rolled from the mouth of the well; then we will water the sheep."

9 While he was still speaking with them, Rachel came with her father's sheep, for she was a shepherd. *10* Now when Jacob saw Rachel, the daughter of Laban, his mother's brother, and the sheep of Laban, his mother's brother, Jacob went up and rolled the stone from the opening of the well, and he watered the sheep of Laban, his mother's brother. *11* Then Jacob kissed Rachel, and lifted his voice and wept. *12* And Jacob told Rachel that he was a relative of her father and that he was Rebekah's son; and she ran and told her father.

13 When Laban heard the news about Jacob, the son of his sister, he ran to meet him; he embraced him and kissed him, and brought him to his house. He told Laban all these things, *14* and Laban said to him, "Surely you are my bone and my flesh!" And he stayed with him a month.

15 Then Laban said to Jacob, "Because you are my relative, should you serve me for nothing? Tell me, what shall your wages be?" *16* Now Laban had two daughters; the name of the older one was Leah, and the name of the younger one was Rachel. *17* Leah's eyes were weak, but Rachel had a beautiful shape and beautiful looks. *18* Jacob loved Rachel; so he said, "I will serve you seven years for Rachel, your younger daughter." *19* Laban said, "It is better that I give her to you than that I should give her to another man. Stay with me." *20* So Jacob served seven years for Rachel, and in his eyes they were like a few days, because of his love for her.

21 Then Jacob said to Laban, "Give me my wife for my time is fulfilled, that I may go in to her." *22* So Laban gathered all the people of the place, and made a feast. *23* But when evening came, he took his daughter Leah and brought her to him; and he went in to her. *24* (Laban had given his maidservant Zilpah to Leah, his daughter, as a maidservant.) *25* Then when morning came, it was Leah! So Jacob said to Laban, "What is this you have done to me? Didn't I serve with you for Rachel? Why did you deceive me!?" *26* Laban said, "This is not done this way in our place—to give the younger girl before the firstborn girl. *27* Complete the week of this one, and we will give you that one also for the service that you will serve with me for yet seven more years." *28* Jacob did so, and completed her week; then he gave to him his daughter Rachel as a wife. *29* (Laban gave to Rachel, his daughter, his maidservant, Bilhah, to be her maidservant.) *30* Then Jacob went in to Rachel also, and he loved Rachel more than Leah. And he served him yet seven more years.

—GENESIS 29:1–30

I COULD INSTANTLY SEE that, while she looked the same, a change had taken place in my sister. Rachel had just come home, running in from the fields. "Where's Father?" she asked breathlessly.

"Still in the fields," I told her. I raised my head from the hearth where I had been busy making bread, and saw my sister leaning against the doorpost for support. She was shaking. I got up and went over to her and took her hands to calm her. Searching her face for a clue, I gently asked what had happened. Rachel was breathing more evenly now and looked directly at me—there was a new light in her dark brown eyes. Her voice was almost a whisper. "Rebekah's son is here."

Rachel then dropped my hands and started pacing around the room. She was speaking so softly to herself that I couldn't understand what she was saying and started to feel agitated. Who was she talking about? Rachel had met a man? He was a relative? We had never met our father's sister Rebekah because she left the family when she was Rachel's age to marry a man who lived far away.[1] Now her son had come? What would that mean for us? Having a visitor was exciting, but why was Rachel so restless about this? Obviously, we just had to tell our father that this man had arrived in Haran.[2] What more did she expect?

Rachel nervously cupped her face with her hands as she continued pacing. I couldn't tell if she was overjoyed or ashamed, then the words came tumbling out . . . something about moving the stone on the well himself? Impossible! It took many men to remove the stone from the well's mouth. He kissed her? He cried! What was she saying?! She continued muttering to herself until she was almost feverish with impatience. Since she wasn't making much sense in this state, we were both relieved to hear the sound of our father's voice in the distance as he came home from the day's work.

Rachel hurried outside to meet him and burst forth with the news: "Jacob has arrived in Haran! Your sister's son is here, by the well!" Curious as to how he would react, I came out of the house and saw our father immediately run to fetch the man, as quickly as I had ever seen him move. When she turned back around to face me, Rachel looked radiant. The agitation was gone; clearly, our father's eagerness to meet his nephew was good news to Rachel. Her eyes glowed, her smile beamed.

"Oh, Leah! I am so happy! Jacob is kind and strong and handsome. He kissed me and wept! I know that we will soon be wed!" I had known Rachel

---

1. In Gen 24, Abraham sends his servant to Haran to procure a wife for his son from his homeland. The servant finds Rebekah, Laban's sister, and brings her back to Canaan to marry Isaac.

2. Haran is located northeast of Israel, toward the top of the Fertile Crescent, on the border of modern day Turkey and Syria. Abraham had settled here on his way from Ur, located on the southern Euphrates, to the land of Canaan (see Gen 11:31).

since the day she was born, but had never seen her act like this. Our mother had died of a fever many years ago when Rachel was barely old enough to start gathering wood. I had become like a mother to Rachel, even though I was just a few years older. Now she was so joyful that it was hard not to react.

But I didn't know what to think. I wanted to hug my sister with happiness and scream at her with anger in the same moment. So I remained silent. Rachel was so wrapped up in her own exhilaration, she barely noticed. Countless thoughts started swimming through my mind: Could she be right? Was it possible that this Jacob would ask for Rachel to be his wife? Did he really kiss her and weep? I wanted to be happy for her, but mostly I was jealous, yet again.

Rachel was the pretty one; everyone said so. Even if no one had said it out loud, how could I not know? We were about the same height; from a distance people often confused us. But once they drew nearer it was clear who had been born with the favor of the gods.[3] Beautiful curvy shape, wavy soft black hair, smooth copper skin, full lips with a quick, inviting smile revealing straight milky-white teeth, and deep, dark, doe-like eyes that lit up her face—all these gifts were Rachel's—as if the gods had kept them from me to save them for her. My small eyes drooped under heavy lids.[4] My teeth were crooked and my hair was like burnt straw, brown and brittle. Young men would look at the two of us and, in same moment, begin ignoring me. What could I do but endure years of being the ugly sister? Yet I always knew that when it came time to be married, it would finally be my turn to be the chosen one. I was the elder daughter and therefore the first wed. This is how I consoled myself through all the years of silent humiliation when people fawned over Rachel's beauty. And now, just because this kinsman had kissed my younger sister, Father was going to allow Rachel to wed first? My heart was pounding and my eyes filled with angry tears.

I glanced at Rachel to see if she noticed, but she was already looking for the servants to tell them to prepare a feast. I tried to stay calm, telling myself that all of this was just Rachel's fantasy. Yet I knew better. Rachel did not lie. My only hope was Father's decision. I kept repeating to myself that

---

3. The family of Laban, like nearly everyone else in the ancient Near East except Abraham, Sarah, and their descendants, would have worshipped many gods. See Gen 31:19.

4. Genesis 29:17 describes Leah's eyes as *rakkôt*, which can be translated as "tender eyed" (KJV), "tender" (ASV), "lovely" (NJB, NRSV), or "delicate" (NKJV). "Weak" (as in the story above) is also a common translation (NAS, NJPS, RSV).

no one in Haran would give their younger daughter to marry before the older one. That's how it worked.

A short while later, the men returned. When Father entered our home, I could see he was also enamored with this visitor. Behind our father came Jacob, also beaming. Everyone was happy but me. I looked him over, this kinsman who had captured my sister's heart, and was struck by his delicate stature. He was of slight but muscular frame with kind, intelligent eyes that were barely darker than his tanned skin. He had a boyish face topped by curly brown hair, and I immediately felt a twinge of feeling for him. When Jacob looked toward me I quickly turned my gaze down for I didn't want him to see my eyes. But Jacob's attention was already on my sister. They were staring at each other openly, as if drawn together by some unseen force. While they stood on opposite sides of the room, Jacob's soft brown irises stared into Rachel's eyes, so dark, but not completely black, like a night full of hope and promises. And she dared to look right back at him! I felt embarrassed. Before she died, our mother had instructed us that a woman should always look down in the presence of a man, an art I had always excelled in.

I pretended to adjust the shoulder of my robe so I would have an excuse not to have to look at them, then left to help the servants prepare the meal. The smell of baked bread wafted into the room, a warm, yeasty aroma filling the air, as if even the food was contributing to their infatuation. I briefly glanced behind me, but they did not seem aware of the smell; all Rachel and Jacob noticed was each other. My retreat helped me hide my red cheeks as my face burned with fury.

I was angry with Rachel. Angry that she had been given such beauty and I wasn't. Angry that Jacob obviously preferred her to me, even though I was more skilled in the arts of the household. Rachel tended sheep, while I ground grain, cooked stew, and wove fabric. I was calm, and controlled the household. Rachel was too restless to be a good wife. She was a shepherd outside all day! She would leave me responsible for the servants and the food while she watched the flocks. It wasn't fair that she got better looks and less responsibility—and now our winsome cousin too!?

These thoughts were tormenting me as I prepared the yogurt for the special meal we would have to honor our guest. I added cucumbers to the yogurt, and even onions for a tart flavor tinged with sweetness. We would dip the bread in the yogurt, complemented by olives, figs, and fresh cheese. Honey wine would enhance this tasty dinner that Jacob could not fail to notice.[5] The family gathered and we ate together. Jacob consumed his food quickly—he was obviously very hungry—and spoke of how delicious it was, the best meal he had had in months. But he looked at Rachel when he said this, of course.

Jacob had been with us for one cycle of the moon when our father told Jacob that they needed to have a talk. Together they went to the fields and stayed there until the sun started to sink. I was working in the house and Rachel had returned from shepherding. Although we didn't speak of the men's conversation, we were both very anxious to know what was being decided. When our father and Jacob came back to the house they were smiling like children. Jacob looked so radiant that I didn't have to ask what had been discussed. When I saw the knowing looks exchanged between Father, Jacob, and Rachel, I was sure. As much as it made my insides ache to admit it, I realized that my little sister would be married before me. Then our father announced that Jacob would stay with us and work for seven years to earn the right to marry Rachel. But he didn't seem to mind.

And so it started. Jacob spent long days working for our father while I had to bear the open adoration that our cousin lavished on my sister. Although Rachel was now staying at home and helping me while Jacob took over the flocks, Jacob sometimes secretly brought her along with him. On those occasions, without Rachel in the house, I would envision her laughing outside with Jacob, which felt worse than witnessing such affection first hand. I kept a stoic demeanor, despite my bitterness that brought tears of frustration to my weak, sad eyes every night.

Seven years went by. Days were filled with hard work but still Jacob seemed increasingly happy. Dulled by the routine over many moons, my jealousy thankfully seemed to fade. As weeks rolled into years, I found myself less enmeshed in a state of constant unease and could finally stop thinking about the imminent humiliation of seeing my little sister wed before me. I felt reborn and started to hope that I would realize my destiny as a woman after all. I started to believe that I could still marry and bear sons for a beloved husband, even if it wasn't this desired cousin.

The day of the wedding eventually arrived. Preparations had been underway for weeks—storing honey, baking cakes, making wine—and now servants were scurrying about carrying jars of almonds, trays of cakes, and jugs of wine. They had set up a new, large tent a bowshot from the house.

5. All of these foods would have been part of the ancient Israelite diet. For detailed discussion, see MacDonald, *What Did the Ancient Israelites Eat?*, 17–40.

This was where Rachel and Jacob would lie together for the first time. Along with the servants, I had spun the wool for this tent, trying not to imagine what would happen beneath its cover. I had forgotten how intensely I had feared this day, but the anticipation of the wedding brought back my dark thoughts. Was I, the unwed older sister, now condemned to remain alone at the service of my father or, worse, serve my married younger sister and her husband? The old jealousy came back and stabbed me in the stomach. I prayed that the gods would create a miracle to free me from this bondage.

And then on the wedding day, a turn of events that I could have never imagined took me by surprise and forever changed my life. The guests came, the music played, the wine flowed. As the merriment continued, my father sought me among the crowd. I turned my head down and adopted a posture of respect, but he took my face between his hands and spoke to me very softly:

"This is for you, Leah. Tonight you will know Jacob and tomorrow you will be husband and wife."

As abruptly as he had approached me, my father departed and left me alone, astonished and confused. Had Father had managed to make Jacob see that he couldn't wed Rachel if I was still unmarried? Had Jacob discovered in all his time with us that this is how things were done in Haran—the firstborn sister was married first? Had he agreed? I watched Father return to the feast and my gaze landed on Jacob. He was laughing and drinking the sweet wine. I felt so happy to be the desired woman for once that I didn't even think about my little sister. I would be the one to marry my father's kinsman, just as my father's sister Rebekah married Isaac when he sent his servant to Haran. I thanked the gods for creating the miracle I had asked for.

One of the maids, Zilpah, came to me, clearly sent by my father, carrying a gown and the bridal veil. I recognized this clothing as the most special garment my mother had ever worn. It was a long-sleeved tunic of fine white wool with a deep purple sash that hugged the waist. I remembered my mother wearing this special dress on festival days, and now it was for my wedding day. The heavy veil had been lying next to it, unworn since our mother's wedding. As Zilpah brushed my hair and put the gown over my head, I felt excitement going through my body. Ziphah told me that she would be my maidservant now. I looked at her and we exchanged a friendly smile. These moments were the beginning of a new, hopeful life.

As I sat still with Zilpah grooming me, my thoughts drifted to Rachel. Of course I felt sorry for her, but she also knew that the older sister married first. It was the right order of things, and she would have to learn to live with it, just as I had lived with seven years of her infatuation. Who knows, maybe with time she could even become happy for me. A nagging voice inside told me this was impossible; my sister clearly loved the man I was about to wed and he loved her too. I knew this. Everyone did. I quickly stopped thinking about it. My happiness and relief were stronger than any guilt. The sound of the drums outside matched my beating heart—but this time it beat with joy, not with jealousy. Zilpah placed the heavy bridal veil on my head and I thankfully noted that my eyes would be hidden.[6] I felt so beautiful.

I got up to leave the house and join the guests in the glow around the fire under the nighttime skies. My father came to me and took my hand to present me as the bride. When the guests saw me approach, the music became louder, the rhythm, faster. I peered out of the side of the veil and there on the far edge of the crowd, I saw Rachel. She was so far back no one noticed her but me. Even from a distance, I could see that my little sister was as sad as I was happy. The look on her face was one that I knew well for I had seen it in my reflection for the last seven years. Resentment? Anger? Hatred? It was the look of someone who has been cheated out of happiness by the person closest to her. Rachel stared at me intently with a look of seething anger, then slipped away into the night darkness.

My gaze trailed after her, as Father held my hand and pulled me toward the center of the crowd. Jacob stumbled toward us. He stood next to my father who put one arm around Jacob's shoulder and called loudly, "More wine for my son-to-be!" Jacob laughed and raised his cup, turning it over to show that it was empty. A servant quickly appeared to refill it with ruby red wine. Jacob playfully lifted the glass to my father and then guzzled its contents in one long drink. "Here is my beautiful daughter," my father said, pushing me toward Jacob. He always called Rachel his beautiful daughter, but what could I do? Here was my one chance for happiness—the guests were gathered—the drums were pounding—the wine was poured—all was happening so quickly—what choice did I have? Jacob raised his cup of wine, once again refilled, first to me then to our guests.

Then came the moments that I both longed for and dreaded. Father led Jacob and me to the tent on the edge of the gathering. Drunken guests called out comments that I pretended not to hear as I lowered my head and

6. Genesis 24:65 suggests that "a woman would wear a veil, sa'ip, to cover her face on her wedding day." Ebeling, *Women's Lives*, 93.

went inside. Jacob staggered into the tent behind me. I knew what was to happen next. My mother had told me about these things before she died, and everyone in the family sleeping in close quarters had left little to the imagination. Jacob would be my husband once I lay with him and I needed to bear sons. Yet I dared to hope that my first night with Jacob would be caring and gentle. I wanted to be touched softly and caressed tenderly. But I was not so fortunate. His movements were quick and hard, his breath coated with alcohol. I felt a stab of pain and it was over. Jacob stopped moving and I turned my head away from his foul odor. He fell asleep quickly afterwards and I lay awake looking at wool I had spun for this tent. This was not the love I had hoped for, but I comforted myself with the assurance that now I had a husband. And I was a wife.

I woke up to the light of the sun peeking through the door flap of the tent. I stayed still and gazed at my husband's sweet face, his delicate jawbone, his high cheekbones. I smiled and put my hand on his cheek. He opened his eyes with a light grin. But when he saw me, his face changed. Jacob sprang up at once, and recoiled from me, a horrified look on his face. He screamed, "I've been tricked!"

Deep down I was not surprised, but I still didn't want to believe it. Of course Jacob had thought I was Rachel all along. Humiliation accompanied realization as I thought back on all the details of the night before: my father's introduction of me as the "beautiful daughter" and Jacob's drunkenness encouraged by my father. I had been tricked too. I had been deceived into thinking that I could be desired, but now I felt more rejected than ever. After last night, I could not have another husband, nor would Jacob ever truly be mine. It didn't matter how many sons I might give him, he would never love me as he loved my younger sister.

Jacob sat up taking in the situation, and became silent. He turned his back to me, his head held in his hands. Then, without a glance in my direction, my husband quickly put on a tunic and rushed out of the tent. I heard him run toward the house, cursing at my father for fooling him. From the tent, I heard all too clearly his accusations coming from the house: "What is this you have done to me? Didn't I serve you for Rachel? Why did you deceive me!?" I lay alone on our wedding bed, and cried bitter, painful tears until I had no more left.

What next? As much as I could not bear the thought of facing anyone in my family, I couldn't stay in the tent forever. Still, I remained there throughout the day, fasting, praying, begging for mercy. Might the gods bestow sons upon me, that I could find some redemption in motherhood?

When the light of day had nearly faded, I readied myself and walked to the house. Rachel was there, her anger still fresh. I had no idea what I could say, but I did not need to worry for she did all the talking. Apparently some negotiations had taken place while I was in the tent. "I will wed him too," Rachel said in a low, angry voice. "Jacob must work longer for Father, but I will marry my husband." She almost spit the words at me.

We had all been cheated. Rachel did not have the husband she wanted. Jacob did not have the wife he wanted. I was the wife who had the husband who did not want me. But Jacob and Rachel's situations would be set right when they wed, and mine would never be. Who was cheated the most?

What about me?

Discussion Questions

1. Do you find Leah a likeable character in this story? Why or why not?

2. Leah seeks status through motherhood, especially through bearing sons. Do you think that this was truly the desire of women or was it more the concern of the Bible writers? Is it possible to know?

3. This story points to difficult dynamics among family members, especially sibling rivalry. What insights about jealousy or how to handle it might we glean from this story?

Bibliography

Ebeling, Jennie R. *Women's Lives in Biblical Times*. London: T & T Clark, 2010.
MacDonald, Nathan. *What Did the Ancient Israelites Eat? Diet in Biblical Times*. Grand Rapids, Mich.: Eerdmans, 2008.

Just before the Abyss

The Legacy of Korah

Joseph A. Ebert

15:32 While the Israelites were in the wilderness, they found a man gathering wood on the Sabbath day. *33* Those who found him gathering wood brought him to Moses, Aaron, and to the whole congregation. *34* They put him under watch, because it was not clear what should be done to him. *35* Then the LORD said to Moses, "The man shall surely be put to death; all the congregation shall pelt him with stones outside the camp." *36* So whole congregation brought him outside the camp and pelted him with stones, and he died, just as the LORD had commanded Moses.

    16:1 Now Korah, son of Izhar son of Kohath son of Levi, took Dathan and Abiram sons of Eliab, and On son of Peleth—descendants of Reuben—*2* and they rose up before Moses with two hundred fifty Israelite men, leaders in the congregation, well-known in the assembly, men of repute. *3* They gathered themselves against Moses and against Aaron, and they said to them, "You have gone too far! For all the congregation is holy, all of them, and the LORD is in their midst. So why do you raise yourselves above the LORD's assembly?" *4* When Moses heard this, he fell on his face. *5* Then he spoke to Korah and all his congregation,[1] saying,

---

1. The NRSV and NJPS render the same Hebrew word *'ēdāh* as "congregation" (NRSV) or "community" (NJPS) when referring to Moses' followers (see Num 16:2, 3, 9, 26 in these translations), but "company" or "band" when referring to those assembled by Korah (see Num 16:5, 6, 11, 16). This shift in word choice subtly downplays the legitimacy of the group that Korah assembles, even though Num 16:2 states that Korah's congregation was made up of well-known, chosen, respected men. The translation above consistently renders *'ēdāh* as "congregation."

"In the morning the LORD will make known who is his, and who is holy, and whom he will let approach him; the one whom he chooses, he will allow to approach him. 6 Do this: take censers for yourselves, Korah and all your congregation, 7 and tomorrow put fire in them, and place incense in them before the LORD; and the man whom the LORD chooses, he will be the holy one. You have gone too far, Levites!" 8 And Moses said to Korah, "Hear now, Levites! 9 Is it too little for you that the God of Israel has separated you from the congregation of Israel, to let you approach him to perform the work of the LORD's tabernacle, and to stand before the congregation and to serve them? 10 He has let you approach, and all your brother Levites with you; and you seek also the priesthood! 11 Therefore you and all your congregation have gathered together against the LORD! Who is Aaron that you complain against him?"

12 Moses sent to call Dathan and Abiram, sons of Eliab; but they said, "We will not come! 13 Is it too little that you brought us up from a land flowing with milk and honey to kill us in the wilderness that you would act like such a prince over us? 14 Also, you did not bring us to a land flowing with milk and honey, or give us an inheritance of a field or a vineyard! Would you gouge out the eyes of these men? We will not come!"

15 Moses was very angry and said to the LORD, "Pay no regard to their offering. I have not taken even one donkey from them, and I have not done evil to one of them." 16 Then Moses said to Korah, "As for you and all your congregation, be present tomorrow before the LORD, you and they and Aaron; 17 and let each man take his censer, and put incense on it, and each man present his censer before the LORD, two hundred fifty censers; you and Aaron, each his censer." 18 So each man took his censer, and they put fire in them and placed incense on them, and they stood at the entrance of the tent of meeting with Moses and Aaron. 19 Korah gathered the whole congregation against them at the entrance of the tent of meeting. Then the glory of the LORD appeared to the whole congregation.

20 And the LORD spoke to Moses and Aaron, saying: 21 "Separate yourselves from the midst of this congregation, for I will annihilate them in a moment!" 22 They fell on their faces and said, "O God, the God of the spirits of all flesh, the one man sins, yet you are angry with the whole

congregation." *23* And the LORD spoke to Moses, saying: *24* "Speak to the congregation, saying: Get away from the dwellings of Korah, Dathan, and Abiram."

25 So Moses got up and went to Dathan and Abiram, and the elders of Israel went after him. *26* He said to the congregation, "Turn away from the tents of these evil men, and do not touch anything of theirs, lest you be swept away for all their sins." *27* So they went away from the dwelling place of Korah, Dathan, and Abiram; and Dathan and Abiram came out and positioned themselves at the entrance of their tents, together with their wives, their children, and their dependents. *28* And Moses said, "By this you will know that the LORD has sent me to do all these deeds, not from my devising: *29* If these people die a death of all humanity, or the fate of all humanity falls to them, the LORD did not send me. *30* But if the LORD creates something new, and the ground opens its mouth and swallows them and all that belongs to them, and they go down alive to Sheol, then you will know that these men have spurned the LORD."

31 As soon as he finished speaking all these words, the ground under them split open. *32* The land opened its mouth and swallowed them and their households—everyone who belonged to Korah and all their possessions. *33* So they, with all that was theirs, went down alive to Sheol; the land covered them, and they perished from the midst of the assembly.

—*NUMBERS 15:32–36; 16:1–33*

THE SKY ABOVE ME is shrinking, minute by ominous minute! In these last horrific moments, my life flashes before me and the events leading up to this end are so clear. Total darkness closes in and all I can see are the terrified faces of those whom I love . . . my wife . . . my children . . . falling . . . . The pain is too much to bear so I turn my thoughts inward as I futilely struggle and wonder, could my end have been any different?

↜

My impending death began with another's. A young man, much beloved in the camp, was murdered for trying to help his family![2] His actions,

2. See Num 15:32–36.

condemned by Moses and Aaron, were necessary. His intentions, regretted by his family, were good. He was punished for his generosity and selflessness; similar efforts that I committed trying to save my people landed me here. Like me, he was a man trying to help those he loved in this barren place. Here in the wilderness, it seems that life is diminished by every act of subsistence. How sadly ironic: Moses, his brother Aaron, and his priests took away the freedom that the Lord had granted us when He took us out of Egypt! It was the Aaronic priesthood that determined what was right and wrong, who was cursed or faultless.[3] They promised us a land flowing with milk and honey, but how is any such promise possible amidst such oppression? I fear that this hope is forever out of reach.

The day when this tragedy began was like all other days—scorching heat with the sun up, bitter cold with the sun down—but this was a day I would never forget. We were cold and needed wood to stay warm, but wood is hard to find in the desert wilderness.

There was a young man whom I admired for his consideration of others. Feeling the chill of the night air on his skin, he searched long and far to find wood for his family. He did not remember that it was the Sabbath, perhaps he did not even know. He thought only of his family staying warm. He worried that his elderly mother, weak and in ill health, might not survive the frigid night. Surely, the preservation of life would outweigh the ruling that gathering wood on the Sabbath is illegal! Certainly, honoring the Lord by honoring the Israelite community was a lawful way of keeping the Sabbath!

Word of the young man's actions quickly reached Moses. I can't imagine much brooding took place before a verdict was reached, because for Moses the law was clear, so he openly declared that the young man's actions were illegal. The ruling: the young man was to be put to death by stoning.

Much to my horror, an assembly quickly gathered just outside the camp to carry out the ruling. Stoning is not a quick way to die, unless the victim is struck in the head by a large stone thrown with great force. The anger of those stoning the condemned person is fortified by common purpose. As the group's sense of self-righteousness grows, so grows the desire to sustain these feelings of violent virtue. There is rarely a single death-imparting blow. Yet the mood is different when the victim is punished

---

3. Exodus 28:30 specifically notes Aaron's authority in making decisions for the community: "In the breastpiece of judgment you shall put the Urim and the Thummim, and they shall be on Aaron's heart when he goes in before the LORD; thus Aaron shall bear the judgment of the Israelites on his heart before the LORD continually" (NRSV).

through a cruel law that lacks justification. As I watched this stoning from a distance, I was filled with despair and anguish. What could I do, as a member of our community was killed with such vindictive violence? My ears rang with his screams of pain. He did not believe that what he had done was contrary to the will of the Lord. Neither did I.

Imagine for a moment the ineffable horror of seeing a loved one murdered for no rational reason, a pawn in a system with no regard for human dignity and worth. Imagine every action as measured and judged, and any deed potentially the last . . .

Days prior to this stoning, I had seen Moses fall on his knees, begging the Lord to spare us for our mistakes.[4] But for some reason this young man's act of kindness toward his kindred merited absolutely no sympathy from our leader. Moses brought us out of Egypt and into this desert. He told us he was going to lead us to the "promised land," to the land of milk and honey, *our inheritance!* But why must so many people die first? And for what? Why did he punish the young man's genuine kindness with this excruciating death? Who is to say that Moses' commands were *from the Lord*? How do we know? How *can* we know?! We followed Moses because we trusted him, but now we suffer from his judgments. We have no way of validating what his ears hear or if what he says is from God or his own mind. We have no means to challenge him or hold him accountable for these increasingly complex commandments, layered with exceptions and incongruities. We had been slaves to Pharaoh. Now we had a new tyrant.

After the stoning, my anger boiled wildly. I feared I wouldn't be able to control my actions. I stalked away, unwilling to witness this execution, afraid of the fury I felt. Would I confront Moses, perhaps violently, before realizing what I had done? These thoughts seethed within me and frightened me as I returned to the camp.

Even in my agitated state, I noticed immediately that an odd feeling had settled over the community. While the thrill of shared anger had fueled the arms of the stoners, the death of this kind man had also fueled many questions about Moses. People were murmuring, "Why did that caring young man have to die?" "Why has Moses turned against us?" "Why do the laws matter to him more than his own people?" The death of a well-meaning soul aroused hatred in the hearts of other benevolent souls. There were rumors that Moses had gone mad. And here, amidst the harsh desert where life is barely tolerable anyway, why should we be ruled by a madman?

4. See Num 14:5, 19.

The quiet murmur of discontent grew into grumblings, then shouts of angered outcry. A crowd gathered and people began shouting for Moses, seeking justice or revenge. I knew that their shouts could be the seed for more violent laws, the "correspondence" between the Lord and Moses, but I joined my voice with theirs. My wife was in the crowd and stood by my side. My anger was almost uncontrollable, and my wife's empathy was invigorating. She too burned within, for she understood what the young man had tried to accomplish that Sabbath day. Our rage ignited against Moses, but he did not appear and eventually the crowd grew tired and dispersed. My fury also began to dissipate, yet I knew that these volatile feelings could easily flare up again.

I decided to gather an assembly of elders to discuss how Moses had betrayed us. Several Reubenites—Dathan and Abiram, sons of Eliab, and On, son of Peleth—met with me between camps.[5] Our people were grumbling, and as leaders of powerful tribes we deserved a say in the laws of the land. Daily, Moses and Aaron brought us increasingly strict laws that determined who was cursed and who was faultless, who would live and who would die. They decided who was worthy of the Lord's favor, who was holy and who was not. Their claimed "favor" with the Lord was manipulative. The young man's death sentence was wicked. Many of us felt this way.

After a few days, my anger receded, replaced with a passionate will to see our community served by justice and freedom. We had been lorded over for too long. I gathered the elders together and we started to make our own decisions. We agreed that the time had come to act, and to act with vigor.

"But how?" a member of the congregation fearfully asked, once we had resolved to do something.

In an attempt to keep the crowd calm, I answered, "We will speak directly with Moses and Aaron, and we will voice our anger. We will approach the holy tabernacle and say, 'No longer will our lives be determined by you two. We are, all of us, holy in the sight of the Lord.' If we want to stay alive, and even prosper in this wilderness, then we must commit ourselves to the lives of each other, and to *forgiveness*. My anger has overrun and exhausted me these past few days. I must commit to the cause of ensuring the freedom of our people."

---

5. Reuben was the oldest son of Jacob and his lineage marks a formidable tribe. Reuben's son, Eliab, was the father of Dathan and Abiram (see Num 26:5–9). This direct lineage from Reuben suggests these men were noted leaders in the community, along with Korah and the Levites.

The gathered elders were a council of 250 well-known leaders who had been appointed by the congregation. Once assembled, we went together to speak to Moses and Aaron, our combined fury growing as we neared the tabernacle. I imagine our approaching footsteps reverberated like those of marching soldiers. Moses no doubt heard us coming because the tabernacle was in clear sight. He and Aaron emerged from the sacred tent of meeting, standing side by side, their eyes filled with contempt. They had heard the grumblings and knew why we had come, but stared at us if we were some petty annoyance. As we got closer, Moses and Aaron stood fast between us and the tabernacle, like a buffer to the Lord.

We stopped a bowshot from Moses and Aaron, our assembly and the tabernacle on either side of the two figures. Despite our large numbers, Moses and Aaron were the center of this drama. For a moment there was almost complete silence. I heard nothing but the pounding of my heart over the soft hot breeze of the desert air. As Moses lifted his hand—no doubt an attempt to demonstrate his authority over us—I stepped forward and cried, "You have gone too far! For all the congregation is holy, all of them, and the Lord is in their midst! So why do you raise yourselves above the Lord's assembly?"[6]

Moses' response was bizarre. But he had heard our grumblings, and so he most assuredly constructed his response to bolster his authority. With intense feeling that he attempted to mask as indifference, he announced, "In the morning, the Lord will make known who is his, and who is holy, and whom he will let approach him. The one whom he chooses, he will allow to approach him. Do this: take censers for yourselves, Korah, and all your congregation, and tomorrow put fire in them, and place incense in them before the Lord.[7] The man the Lord chooses will be the one who is holy. You have gone too far, Levites!"

The suggestion that we Levites could prepare the censer, a ritual object, was improper; we had our own regulated priestly duties. Our responsibilities included furnishing the tabernacle and leading services, but not making ritual preparations or offerings.[8] For Moses, Aaron is the high priest, the only person the Lord would draw near to him.[9] Moses' suggestion for

6. Num 16:3. Much of the ensuing dialogue in this story comes from Num 16:4–30.

7. Censers were "hand-held devices in which incense was placed along with burning coals," used primarily by priests during religious rituals. Meyers, "Censers," n.p., *ABD on CD-ROM*.

8. While the Bible describes the Levites as a priestly tribe, the implications of this designation vary in different texts. See Powell, "Levites," 556.

9. For discussion of Aaron's exalted role as a leader, see Spencer, "Aaron," n.p., *ABD*

us to bring censers was meant to belittle us and remind us what we could and could not do within the Israelite community.[10] There was no doubt in my mind that Moses was taking advantage of an ill-formed priestly organization and defining it on his own terms with a clear structure to benefit himself and his brother. The test Moses offered was not given by God, but was constructed by a man for his brother in order to elevate their station. That he was attempting to hide his bias with a rigged contest instead of with diplomacy became clear with his next declaration:

"Hear now, Levites! Is it too little for you that the God of Israel has separated you from the congregation of Israel, to let you approach him to perform the work of the Lord's tabernacle, and to stand before the congregation and to serve them? He has let you approach, and all your brother Levites with you, *and you seek also the priesthood!* Therefore, you and all your congregation have gathered together against the Lord! Who is Aaron that you complain against him?"

Clearly, we could not trust Moses. He knew that our cause was greater than the priesthood. We wanted to connect to the Lord directly, rather than through Moses' biased voice and dubious actions. But in an effort to side-step the intentions of the congregated people, Moses summoned Dathan and Abiram separately, imploring them to give up their cause.[11] This endeavor was a deceitful attempt to place responsibility for this rebellion solely upon me. However, the real blame for the tension and division in the community belonged not on me, or on us, the people of the Lord, but on Moses and his power-hungry intentions.

Before Moses could single me out, Dathan and Abiram defied Moses. "We will not come! Is it too little that you brought us up from a land flowing with milk and honey to kill us in the wilderness that you would act like such a prince over us? Also, you did not bring us to a land flowing with milk and honey, or give us an inheritance of a field or a vineyard! Would you gouge out the eyes of these men? We will not come!"

Clearly feeling he had lost his authority, Moses fell on his knees and looked up toward the sky and screamed, "Pay no regard to their offering.

---

on CD-ROM.

10. Although both Korah and Aaron are descended from the priestly tribe of Levi (Exod 4:14; Num 16:1), the Bible repeatedly notes the tension between the Aaronite and Levitical priesthoods, as reflected in Num 16 (see also Exod 32:25–35). Texts from the Priestly source portray Aaron and his descendants as the only legitimate priests to perform religious rites in the temple (see Lev 6:8–9:24; Num 3:1–10; 18:1–7.). Ibid.

11. See Num 16:12.

I have not taken even one donkey from them, and I have not done evil to one of them!"

I faced Moses and stood tall, my feet rooted in the sand, and shot back, "You have taken a beloved and generous member of our community! Why do you speak about a donkey? Was this young man whom you had stoned not a member of the Israelite community? Did he not deserve mercy and forgiveness?"[12] Exhausted from anger, I collapsed to my knees. With my head slung low, my chin resting deep on my chest, I lamented, "You have taken so much from us, as you continue to do. What would you have us do?" I looked up at Moses and implored, "What would *the Lord* have us do?"

Moses was firm and reiterated his earlier instructions. "As for you and all your congregation, be present tomorrow before the Lord, you and they and Aaron; and let each man take his censer, and put incense in it, and each man present his censer before the Lord, two hundred fifty censers; you and Aaron, each his censer."

So I was to go up with my people against Aaron. It occurred to me that these commandments were merely coming from Moses. He had no idea what else to propose, which is why he repeated the same instructions. I would call his bluff. We would take on the ritualistic duties and he would see how capable we were. Moses would then need to recognize our authority. We could change these vindictive laws. We would create a way to abide in the peace of justice, not tyranny.

And so I assembled all 250 of my congregation and we gathered at the entrance to the tent of meeting. The sun beat down as we made our way to the tabernacle. Our sandals disturbed the sand, so hot it nearly scalded our feet. Heat came up from the earth, beat down from the sun, rose from our hands holding the burning censers. Incense, fire, and smoke made it hard to see, and with all the heat it was even hard to breathe. With so many censers burning, clouds from the incense drifted above our congregation; from a distance it must have appeared as if there were a great fire. The incense manifested our frustration, as the symbol of our protest burned. There had been enough feuding, enough anger, enough sadness. The time had come to determine the fate of the Israelite community.

I never wanted anyone else to die. I certainly did not want to lead my family to this sure death. I simply wanted to remember that gentle young man, and let the community know that he was worth more than a donkey. I

---

12. This statement from Korah diverges from the biblical text, although the next declaration from Moses reverts to Num 16:16–17.

wanted the congregation to realize that each and every Israelite was valued beyond measure. Only the Lord could determine our worth.

After the smoke from the incense had cleared, the agitation of our assembly cooled down as the sun started to slip in the sky. No longer slaves, we craved the freedom to live in safety, not fearing our leader. Eventually, silence, instead of smoke, filled the air. Time joined sound in ceasing, as though something fierce was waiting to wake up.

Then—in a flash—the glory of the Lord appeared before us! In this bright and searing light, silence was ripped from space. With piercing intensity, my body—both hot and cold—writhed uncontrollably! My existence felt obliterated to a blank nothingness. I could see nothing. I couldn't feel the sand beneath me. I couldn't see through the murky opacity of the space that engulfed me. All was gone, yet I still existed. For a second I was elevated in some otherworldly place, alone in a gray void.

From no discernible location, a deep and reverberating voice rang out, "Separate yourselves from the midst of this congregation, for I will annihilate them in a moment!" Who was speaking? And to whom?! Was the voice talking to me, Dathan, and Abiram about Moses and Aaron, or was the voice talking to them about us?

Moses quickly spoke up. "O God, the God of the spirits of all flesh, the one man sins, yet you are angry with the whole congregation." The Lord was not talking to me. My heart dropped within my chest and broke as I felt overwhelmed with sadness. I knew I had lost something indescribable yet infinite. The Lord seemed so close in that voice and yet remained so unreachably far away from me. The God I sought to follow had turned against me and was emptying my total being—heart, mind, and body. And I felt and understood the meaning of meaninglessness.

The deep voice continued and rumbled through my broken core, instructing Moses: "Speak to the congregation saying, 'Get away from the dwellings of Korah, Dathan and Abiram!'" Then I knew that the lives of the Israelite community, like the young man's life, were beyond my control, even beyond the control of Moses and Aaron. Life and its worth were not for me to determine. The freedom we had gained from our treacherous exodus had convinced me that our God cared about us. I had thought our lives were our own, but in this searing moment I realized that I was wrong. Suddenly, the light that had overwhelmed me, separating me from the world I had known, dissipated, and the earth below me began to tremble.

A sound—an otherworldly screech accompanied by a dark and fearsome roar—penetrated my being. My fate was unthinkable; I was unthinkable.

The earth has opened up and I am falling ever downward. I can see the sky above me, but only darkness below me. I hear the screams of those I loved, my family and friends. They are falling with me, because they too believed in our cause; they too are now consumed by darkness. Terror and despair burst from their lungs as their screams pierce the murky air.

I brought us here. Moses couldn't have saved us, just as he couldn't have saved the young man. But I realize now—too late—that the tyrant is the Lord.

The light is almost gone as thick darkness surrounds us. Below, I sense a flickering glow emanating from the bowels of the earth. Through the cold emptiness of this abysmal blackness, I hear dreadful screams in the distance . . . how far away I cannot be certain . . . the darkness is too deep. These screams are more grotesque, more horrifying.

Dear God! They're burning alive!!!

Forgive me, Lord.

Forgive me . . .

Discussion Questions

1. What do you think of Korah in Numbers 16? Does the biblical text suggest he is a leader trying to speak up for his people or an inciter of unnecessary rebellion? Do any contemporary figures come to mind when you think of Korah?

2. This story shows Moses as unfair and God as a tyrant. Can the biblical text in Numbers 15–16 sustain such an interpretation? Why do we resist seeing Moses and God in this way?

3. At the end of the story, Korah feels that he was wrong to think that he was in control of his own life. Do you ever sense that you are not in control of your own life? In those situations, what choices could you have, if any?

Bibliography

Meyers, Carol. "Censers." In ABD on CD-ROM.

Powell, Mark Allan, ed. HarperCollins Bible Dictionary. 3rd ed. New York: HarperCollins, 2011.

Spencer, John. "Aaron." In ABD on CD-ROM.

Only Hope

A Prequel to Judges 19

SARAH CONDON

1 In those days, when there was no king in Israel, a Levite, residing in the remote parts of Mount Ephraim, took for himself a concubine from Bethlehem in Judah. *2* His concubine became angry with him[1] and she went from his house to the house of her father, in Bethlehem of Judah; and she was there for four months. *3* Then her husband got up and went after her to speak to her, to bring her back. (His servant was with him and a pair of donkeys.) She brought him into her father's house, and when the girl's father saw him he rejoiced to meet him.

4 His father-in-law, the girl's father, grasped him and he stayed with him three days; they ate and drank and slept there. *5* On the fourth day they arose early in the morning and got up to go. But the girl's father said to his son-in-law, "Sustain your heart with a morsel of bread, and afterward you may go." *6* So they stayed and the two of them ate and drank together. Then the father of the girl said to the man, "Please, wouldn't you like to sleep? It will be good for you." *7* But the man got up to go, so his father-in-law pressed upon him, then he stayed and he slept there. *8* He arose early in the morning to go on the fifth day, and the girl's father said, "Please, sustain yourself." So they lingered until the day's decline and the two of them ate. *9* Then the man got up to go, he and his concubine and his servant. The father of the girl said to his son-in-law,

---

1. The translation of this verse follows the Septuagint (i.e., the Greek translation of the Hebrew Scriptures); see also the RSV and NRSV.

"Look, the day is sinking into evening. Please sleep and settle down here today; it will be good for you. Tomorrow you can arise early for your journey and go to your dwelling place."

10 But the man did not want to stay the night. He got up and he left and he came to the front of Jebus (that is, Jerusalem). With him was a pair of saddled donkeys, and his concubine was with him. *11* They were near Jebus and the day was done. The servant said to his master, "Please, come and let us turn aside to this city of the Jebusites so we can sleep there." *12* But his master said to him, "We will not turn aside to a city of strangers who are not from among the children of Israel, but we will pass on to Gibeah." *13* He said to his servant, "Come and we will get near to one of the places, then we will lodge in Gibeah or in Ramah." *14* So they crossed over and they went. The sun went down on them near Gibeah, which belongs to Benjamin.

15 So they turned aside there to go to lodge in Gibeah. He came in and sat in the square of the city, but no one took them in to lodge. *16* In the evening, an old man was coming from his work in the field. (The man was from Mount Ephraim and he was residing in Gibeah; the people in the place were Benjaminites.) *17* He looked up and saw the wayfarer in the square of the city. The old man said, "Where have you come from and where are you going?" *18* He said to him, "We are passing over from Bethlehem in Judah to the remote parts of Mount Ephraim. I am from there and I went to Bethlehem in Judah and am going to the house of the Lord, but no one has offered to take me in. *19* There is straw and fodder for our donkeys, and also bread and wine for me, your maidservant, and the lad with your servants. There is no shortage of anything." *20* The old man said, "Peace be with you. I will take care of all your needs, only do not spend the night in the square." *21* He took him to his house and mixed fodder for the donkeys. Then they washed their feet and ate and drank.

22 They were making their hearts merry when men of the town—worthless men—surrounded the house, and started pounding on the door. They called to the old man, the owner of the house, "Bring out the man who came to your house so we can have sex with him." *23* The owner of the house went out and said to them, "No my brothers, do not do this evil against this man who has come to my house. Do not do this disgraceful thing! 24 Here is my virgin daughter and his concubine; I will bring them out to you. Rape them and do to them whatever seems good to you, but do not do this disgraceful thing to this man!" 25 But the men were not willing to listen to him. So the man grabbed his concubine and put her to them outside. They raped her and abused her all night until morning. Then they cast her off when dawn arose.

26 As morning came, the woman came and fell at the door of the man's house where her master was, until it became light. 27 When her master got up in the morning, he opened the door the house and went out to go on his way. There was his concubine fallen at the entrance to the house with her hands on the threshold. 28 He said to her, "Get up. Let's go." But there was no answer. He put her on his donkey, and he got up and went to his place. 29 When he came to his house, he took the knife and grabbed his concubine and cut her to her bones in twelve pieces. Then he sent her to all the territory of Israel. 30 And all who saw her said, "Never has such a thing as this happened or been seen since the days when the Israelites came up from the land of Egypt until today. Set your hearts on her, take counsel, and speak."[2]

—JUDGES 19:1–30

I REMEMBER WHEN THE children were small, they would fall fast asleep within minutes of us lying down, all tuckered out from a long day's work. My husband Ben and I used to lie awake, looking at the stars, and whispering about how good Yahweh had been to us.[3] As the oldest son, Ben had inherited his family's plot of land, right near Bethlehem. Our land is fertile and well-suited for wheat, which the family has grown there from generation to generation. We also had a few goats and one white sheep with soft,

2. For discussion of women and dismemberment in ancient Near Eastern texts, see Parker, "Remembering the Dismembered," 174–90.

3. Families in the land of Canaan during the Iron Age (1200–587 BCE), when this story is set, generally lived in small open-air compounds of houses. Most houses had four small rooms and two stories, with a flat roof on top. The family's few sheep and/ or goats would be kept in the house at night. People often slept on the roof to get some distance from the smell and sound of animals below. For a fictitious account of a girl's life in ancient Israel, see Parker, "You Are a Bible Child," 60–63.

fluffy wool.[4] Our family had been larger, but that changed quickly many seasons ago. Ben's parents died suddenly from the consuming fever that also took his brother and sent his young bride back to her father's house for another husband. With fewer hands, the work was relentless, but so far we had managed to get by. I would listen to sweet Ben talk, smelling of dirt and sweat, as our children slept. Our precious Abia and Dov. Of the four children I carried, two of them survived and we prayed that their lives would always be secure.

As a mother I had done all that I could to prepare Abia for marriage. In marrying my own dear Ben I had been so lucky; I only hoped that Abia would have the same fortune. And why wouldn't she? Abia was a strong and beautiful girl. By the time she was five she was able to carry the water up from the cisterns all by herself.[5] I still remember beaming with pride as I watched her haul the jug up the hill. Last harvest season, when the flow of blood first came from her, she grew even stronger as her body blossomed with new shape and promise. Her skin glowed like honey and her dark hair was long and flowing like a river at night. When she smiled, her eyes looked like dancing stars. I knew we would find a good match for her.

If I remember correctly, Abia was around 13 and Dov was about 15 when a dark cloud began to slide over our lives. The darkness first descended on Dov's big brown eyes. It was his father who first noticed the redness in Dov's eyes as they were working in the fields together. Ben was sure it would go away—but it did not. Dov's eyes grew blurry from his view and from ours. They seemed to recede into his face.[6] When Dov could no longer see anything, we knew our hope for the future was in trouble.

Our plans had to change radically. We always thought that Dov would marry one of the girls in our family's clan. For a boy, he was still young to marry so we had not started to look for a wife.[7] No promises had been

4. Wheat was a common field crop in ancient Israel. Most people farmed their family plot of land and had a few small cattle, such as sheep and goats, which were cheaper to feed and keep than cows. See Jacob and Jacob, "Flora," and Firmage, "Zoology," n.p., *ABD on CD-ROM.*

5. Bethlehem does not have any natural springs, only cisterns (i.e., large holes carved in rock to capture rain water). Cazelles, "Bethlehem" n.p., *ABD on CD-ROM.*

6. Blindness was a common condition due to poor hygiene and disease-carrying flies. (This disease that causes blindness is now called trachoma and is curable with proper medical care.) Trachoma often leads to lid deformities over time. Sussman, "Sickness and Disease," n.p., *ABD on CD-ROM.*

7. Boys married later than girls, often in their early 20's. The betrothal of a woman to a man was a serious arrangement, nearly as binding as a marriage. King and Stager, *Life*

made for marriage and so there were none to be broken. I tried to see that as a blessing. It seems that the only thing that would break poor Dov's heart more than losing his sight would be for a girl's family to feel forced to break a promise of marriage.

Ben and I had always had enough to get by, plus a small amount of stored goods. We knew from experience that we could survive one bad crop. We had never had to know about getting through more than that. But the year that Dov went blind was followed by two years of little water from the sky.[8] Abia, Ben, and I would take turns gathering water from the cisterns and tediously walking from one dried out plant to another, sprinkling precious drops, willing the seeds to grow. Between Dov's swollen useless eyes and the sad stubs of young wheat plants, it felt like our world was dying. Everyone we knew was in the same situation, watching the hopes for their family wither. All of those nights that Ben and I had spent talking about Dov taking over the family plot and guiding us through our old age seemed like unreachable dreams. How would he marry a good woman now? What could he do to feed himself as we got older?

We had built up some reserves of food but they were wearing down. We still had fodder for the animals; in time we would be eating it ourselves. It was becoming increasingly hard for all of us to make it. There just wasn't enough.

And that is when Tal, the Levite, came into our lives. He was on his way from Mount Ephraim and stopped in to ask for a night's lodging. Ben and I had always done our best to train the children to welcome strangers. As fate would have it, Abia was on her way back from the cistern with a jug full of water. I used to tease Abia and tell her that she would meet her husband bringing water back from the well. After all, the great love affair of Rachel and Jacob happened in a similar fashion.[9] Of course, I had only been jesting. We had always planned on finding her a good match, and to make sure she was well cared for and happy. That had all changed. My little joke was no longer funny.

Abia ran inside where I was grinding wheat to tell me we had a visitor and that he wished to stay with us. I sent her out into the fields to tell Ben. We met in front of the house just in time to greet Tal. He was a tall man,

---

in Biblical Israel, 54.

8. Drought was a common problem in ancient Israel; only two years of no rain could drive a farm into ruin. Blenkinsopp, "Family in First Temple Israel," 55.

9. See Gen 29:1–12.

bigger than my Ben and certainly larger than Dov. He smelled like incense and oil.[10] When he spoke his voice had a simple authority:

"I am a traveling Levite on my way to the temple. Can I spend a night or two with your family?"

"Of course!" Ben insisted.

This was the obvious response since we know that it is our responsibility to take care of a traveler.[11] Still, the timing could not have been worse. Rainfall was still a problem and the little food we had was dwindling. I knew Ben; he would give whatever we had to the traveler, not only for the night, but to take with him. What could I do? I told Abia to walk Tal out to the cisterns so his donkey could get water.

"Pull out the best we have!" Ben barked at me.

"The best we have?" I asked incredulously. "But we hardly have anything."

Ben grasped my hands and loudly whispered, "Don't you see Sarah? This man might take our Abia for his own! He looks like he has enough and could take care of her."

"What will we do without her?"

I did not want to admit it, even to myself, but I was starting to feel a bit weak. I was deathly afraid the consuming fever might reach me too and I needed her help. I was not ready to give up my hard-working girl.[12]

"Sarah, you must think about what's best for Abia. She could make a life for herself and have more than we could give her."

"But surely he's married." Slowly I looked at Ben with shock and hurt in my eyes. "Are you saying Abia would be his concubine?"[13]

"Do you know how lucky we are, Sarah? You and I have never even seen a Levite!"[14]

10. The Levites were a priestly tribe and would have offered incense as part of their ritualistic duties. Nielsen, "Incense," n.p., *ABD on CD-ROM.*

11. Caring for the wellbeing and safety of a guest was an important responsibility in ancient Israel. The host would eagerly greet and welcome the visitor into his home. See Borowski, *Daily Life in Biblical Times,* 22–24.

12. Agricultural work would have been performed by men, women, and children, all of whom contributed labor in the constant struggle for survival. Meyers, "Family in Early Israel," 23.

13. A concubine had lower status than other women. A wife produced an heir and a concubine was for sexual pleasure. For discussion see Bellis, *Helpmates, Harlots, and Heroes,* 118.

14. Based on Judges 17–18, the presence of Levites in a household would have been very unusual during this time. They did not grow in prominence until their numbers increased and they were allowed to work at local sanctuaries. Rehm, "Levites," n.p., *ABD*

"So we can only hope that he will treat her well," I replied flatly.

"A Levite's concubine is certainly better than a starving girl from Bethlehem. It's the only hope for *her*."

I could not respond to this. After all those years of raising Abia and wanting the best for her, this was almost too much to bear. She was to be a first wife, a real wife, not someone's concubine. I had spent hours sitting with Abia while we made bread, talking with her about all that would be expected of her as a wife in her own household.[15] And still, there was a more selfish part of me that didn't want to see my daughter go. At just fourteen, she was barely ready for the responsibilities of a wife, much less a concubine.

"But she's so young, Ben. How can we just send her off with this man?"

"Maybe . . ." Ben answered slowly; I could see that he was thinking. He added, "Maybe we can get them to stay here, to move here, with us."

Of course! What a hopeful man I had married. We have a house and fields. This could be the base for Tal the Levite. He could have all the prestige of the priesthood and some stability. Surely, as Abia's parents and the proper owners of the house, we would be allowed to stay in our own home. Maybe we could build a house for his family next door! Just imagine all the time I would have left with my sweet Abia. Maybe even the rains would come back. Maybe Ben and I wouldn't die with only a blind son to worry over. We would have grandchildren to take care of us! Tal could be the answer to everything . . . and then, reality began to settle in.

I faced Ben, "Could this really work?"

"Sarah," he said firmly, "we have been losing so much for so long. Doesn't it just feel good to hope again?"

Ben was right. It did feel good to hope. That night I gathered what I had to make the best meal I possibly could. This was the food of wooing and I needed it to do its job. I wanted Tal to see how well he would eat if he moved in with us, and to think of the delicious food that our Abia could prepare. I managed to pull together some pita bread and some yogurt I had made the day before. A few years ago, when we traded several bushels of wheat for a goat, I never imagined I would be using her milk to prepare such an important meal. In addition to the yogurt and pita, we had some leeks from my garden in the back. We still had a few jugs of wine from

---

on CD-ROM.

15. The processing of grains took hours to complete. The grains would have to be soaked, milled, and ground before they could be incorporated into dough and made into bread. Meyers, "Family in Early Israel," 25.

trading a small lamb. I brought out one jug that we kept in the back of the house, knowing this would help. Any other year I would have had so much more to offer our guest. Still, I took great pride in the yogurt I made and hoped that it would be to Tal's liking. It seemed best that Ben and Tal sit down and discuss this arrangement together at dinner. That gave me a chance to explain to Abia what might happen.

I found myself envious of Ben. As difficult as it might have been for him to offer our whole home to a stranger, I had to explain to Abia why we were offering her as well.

"Do you know how I have told you that someday you will be like me? Someday you will have your own family and husband to feed, and nurture, and care for?"

"Yes Mama."

"Well, your father is talking to Tal about being your husband."

"But Mama, he is as old as Papa! And I thought I would be a little older! Will I have to leave you now?"

Abia began to cry. I put her head in my lap, ran my fingers through her dark hair, and was reminded that she had so recently crested womanhood. I explained to Abia that we had hoped Tal would want to move back to where we are and that we would not be parting ways permanently. I told her she might be with us for years to come. She seemed calmed by this. I could only hope that Tal's family would treat her well and that Tal's wife would see my Abia as a good worker.

Considering Tal's role as a Levite, I had high hopes for the way he would treat my daughter. Surely he wouldn't expect her to lay with him right away. What I didn't tell Abia was about being Tal's concubine. I couldn't begin to explain to her that she would be asked to have sex with him. Abia was old enough to know what her father and I did under the cover of night, but certainly not old enough for it to be expected of her. It seemed best that she just experience what life would be like with this new man. Maybe she could even find some pride. For years now I had taught Abia how to make baskets. She also had an undeniable knack for weaving cloth. Maybe one of those skills could serve her. I told myself that her work would be rewarded, and just maybe it would be here with us.[16] With those comforting thoughts

16. In addition to agricultural work, women also cared for their children, prepared meals, produced textiles, and kept the household running. Whereas sons would spend time with both parents, daughters would likely spend nearly all of their premarital years at their mother's side, creating a close bond. Meyers, "Family in Early Israel," 25, 38.

I put Abia to bed and explained to her that this would all look better in the morning.

I lay on the roof for hours hearing Tal and Ben talk over food and drink. Over the hiss of the fire, I could not understand what they were saying but Tal seemed to be laughing a great deal. I took that to be a good sign. Eventually, Ben came up and lay next to me. He pressed his face, still warm from the fire, on mine.

"Sarah, are you awake?" he whispered.

"Yes Ben, I'm awake."

"Well, he is married."

"Of course! He's practically your age."

"But," Ben offered, "he will take Abia as his concubine. Obviously, there would be no bride payment.[17] He told me we are just lucky that he can take her off our hands."

"Did he promise to come back here?" I asked.

"He said he might consider it."

I found hope in Ben's words and rose early that morning to plan what I needed to gather for Abia's journey. I was worried. Never having traveled before myself, I didn't really know how to prepare my daughter. I hoped that Tal would be patient with her and protect her. The only thing I knew about being on the road was that it was dangerous. I just wanted my little Abia to be safe. Ben told me that with the lack of rain, the roads would be dusty.[18] I tucked a few tattered cloths into Abia's bag so that she could cover her face. There was pita leftover from Ben's dinner with Tal so I carefully wrapped that in with her belongings. I had one special item to send with her: my colorful linen garment. Unlike the coarse, natural tunics we usually wore, this large piece of fabric was soft. I did my best not to wear it too much, putting it on only for celebrations. My own mother had given it to me when I left her household at Abia's age, and that was the last time I saw her. Despite the mended holes it had acquired over the years, and the vibrant red fabric now faded to pink, this garment was still the nicest thing

---

17. Normally, a future son-in-law would pay the father of the betrothed girl a *mōhar* or bride-price. This gift would compensate the household for the loss of the daughter. King and Stager, *Life in Biblical Israel*, 54.

18. Roads were often dangerous, with difficult terrain to navigate and threats from animals and people. Even major roads would have been hampered by mud in the wet seasons and dust in the dry, hot months. Beitzel, "Travel and Communication" n.p., *ABD on CD-ROM*.

I owned. It seemed only appropriate to send it with Abia. I decided to show her how to wear it, so I nudged her awake.

"Abia, wake up and come outside," I whispered.

"Is it happening Mama? Am I leaving?" she whispered back.

"Yes Abia," I said, trying to sound cheerful. "Now come outside."

Of all the times I had imagined preparing to send Abia off with the man she would spend the rest of her life with, this was not how I had thought it would be.

"Abia, I want you to have this wrap that belonged to my mother. Let me show you how to use it."

Considering how small Abia was, I had to fold the cloth over by a third. Then I was able to wrap the fabric around her and fit it over her shoulder.[19]

"There," I said, "you look beautiful."

I meant it. And she could stay strong and beautiful since Tal was willing to provide for her. I just had to keep reminding myself of this. I showed Abia the satchel I had packed for her, explained to her how to use the cloths to protect her face, and instructed her to put on this wrap when she met Tal's family. I wanted to tell her not to be scared. But I kept that part to myself. There wasn't time. Everything about that morning felt so rushed, but most especially the moments I had left with my daughter.

"Let's go wake up your brother so you can tell him goodbye."

The previous night I had quietly told Dov what our plan was after Abia had fallen asleep. He was so upset with us. Dov was old enough to know what would be expected of his sister and was not nearly as hopeful as his father and I were. After Abia came down from waking Dov up, I sent her out to the cisterns to get water for her journey.

Dov's disfigured, blind face appeared in front of mine and demanded, "Have you told her yet, Mama? Have you told her what a concubine does? Have you told her she won't really be a wife?"

"Of course not, Dov!" I hissed. "That will only scare her. Besides, there might be a chance that she'll come back."

"Mama," he said intently, "she's not coming back."

"Dov, this is the only option we have. If the lack of rain continues we will all starve. You know that. Now go inside and keep away. You're not helping."

19. Archeological evidence suggests that women may have worn colorful garments wrapped around the body with one edge thrown over her left shoulder. Edwards, "Dress and Ornamentation" n.p., *ABD on CD-ROM*.

As I watched Dov awkwardly make his way back into the house, I wondered if he might be right. Life would be so different for our Abia. Just then, Tal appeared out of his tent and yelled at me:

"Does the boy have a problem with my arrangement for his sister? What kind of household do you run with children talking like that?"

I was not prepared for him to be so aggressive and I suddenly felt defensive about my children. Then I remembered how this man might be the only hope for our daughter. I swallowed my pride and lowered my eyes.

Tal put his head down and said darkly, "We're going to have real problems if your daughter does not know her place." Immediately I realized what was at stake here. If we wanted Tal to take Abia, and more importantly, if we wanted him to return, I had to make certain he knew that this was a good deal for him.

"You are right about this," I lied.

"Fine," he grunted. "Get the girl and her things together. I want to leave before dark."

Unable to contain myself, I ventured to ask Tal about his plans for the future.

"Do you have any idea if you'll return?" I tried not to sound desperate.

"Well I'm back and forth to Ephraim. And there's a tent in Bethel where my wife lives.[20] Your home is obviously much nicer and you have a decent plot of land. But as much as I'd be gone from here, I'd need to know I was in charge. Your boy does not know when to keep his mouth shut. He's blind, isn't he?"

"Yes," I said, and held my breath.

"Well, maybe he won't be around much longer."

Hot tears of anger filled my eyes. I said nothing.

As I hurried inside to gather more food for Abia's journey, I could feel a horrible pit in my stomach. Suddenly, it felt like everything we had worked for was being ripped away. What if we were making a terrible mistake? What if Tal was an awful man? But this seems our best option and it might make everything better.

So for now, as I send my daughter off, I can only hope.

---

20. Since Levites did not hold familial lands, their families would likely dwell in tents. Aschkenasy, *Woman at the Window*, 64.

Discussion Questions

1. Many people are not familiar with Judges 19 and the story of the Levite's concubine. Are you surprised that it is in the Bible? How does this story about Abia influence your understanding of the biblical text?

2. The mother in this story is faced with hard choices. What do you think you would have done in her situation?

3. Can this difficult Bible story be used to help people who experience sexual violence? If so, how? If not, why not?

Bibliography

Aschkenasy, Nehama. *Woman at the Window*. Detroit: Wayne State University Press, 1998.

Beitzel, Barry J. "Travel and Communication." In *ABD on CD-ROM*.

Bellis, Alice Ogden. *Helpmates, Harlots, and Heroes: Women's Stories in the Hebrew Bible*. Louisville, Ky.: Westminster John Knox, 2007.

Blenkinsopp, Joseph. "The Family in First Temple Israel." In *Families in Ancient Israel*, edited by Leo G. Perdue, Joseph Blenkinsopp, John J. Collins, and Carol Meyers, 48–103. Louisville, Ky.: Westminster John Knox, 1997.

Borowski, Oded. *Daily Life in Biblical Times*. Atlanta: Society of Biblical Literature, 2003.

Cazelles, Henry. "Bethlehem." In *ABD on CD-ROM*.

Edwards, Douglas R. "Dress and Ornamentation." In *ABD on CD-ROM*.

Firmage, Edward. "Zoology." In *ABD on CD-ROM*.

Jacob, Irene and Walter Jacob. "Flora." In *ABD on CD-ROM*.

King, Philip J. and Lawrence E. Stager. *Life in Biblical Israel*. Louisville, Ky.: Westminster John Knox, 2001.

Meyers, Carol. "The Family in Early Israel." In *Families in Ancient Israel*, edited by Leo G. Perdue, Joseph Blenkinsopp, John J. Collins, and Carol Meyers, 1–46. Louisville, Ky.: Westminster John Knox, 1997.

Nielsen, Kjeld. "Incense." In *ABD on CD-ROM*.

Parker, Julie Faith. "You are a Bible Child: Exploring the Lives of Children and Mothers through the Elisha Cycle." In *Women in the Biblical World: A Survey of Old and New Testament Perspectives*, edited by Elizabeth A. McCabe, 59–69. Lanham, Md.: University of America Press, 2009.

———. "Remembering the Dismembered: Piecing Together Meaning from Stories of Women and Body Parts in Ancient Near Eastern Literature." *Biblical Interpretation* 23 (2015) 174–190.

Rehm, Merlin D. "Levites." In *ABD on CD-ROM*.

Sussman, Max. "Sickness and Disease." In *ABD on CD-ROM*.

The Outing

Emily Phillips Lloyd

1 Solomon allied himself by marriage alliance with Pharaoh, king of Egypt; he took Pharaoh's daughter and brought her into the city of David, until he finished building his own house and the house of the Lord and the wall surrounding Jerusalem.

16 Later, two women, prostitutes, came to the king and stood before him. *17* The one woman said, "Oh, my lord, this woman and I live in the same house; and I gave birth with her in the house. *18* Then on the third day after I gave birth, this woman also gave birth. We were together; there was no stranger with us in the house, just the two of us were in the house. *19* And this woman's son died in the night, because she lay on him! *20* So she got up in the middle of the night and took my son from beside me while your servant slept. She laid him at her breast, and she laid her dead son at my breast. *21* When I got up in the morning to nurse my son—he was dead! But when I looked closely at him in the morning, clearly it was not my son that I had borne." *22* But the other woman said, "No! My son is alive and your son is dead!" The first said, "No, because your son is dead, and my son is alive!" So they argued before the king.

23 Then the king said, "The one says, 'My son is alive and your son is dead!' And that one says, 'No! Because your son is dead and my son is alive!' *24* So the king said, "Bring me a sword." And they brought the sword before the king. *25* The king said, "Divide the living child in two;

then give half to one, and half to the other." 26 Then the woman whose son was alive said to the king—because compassion for her son burned within her—"Oh, my lord, give her the living boy; certainly do not kill him!" The other said, "It shall be neither for me or for you—Divide it!" 27 Then the king responded and said, "Give her the living child; certainly do not kill him. She is his mother."

28 And all Israel heard of the judgment that the king had judged; and they were in awe of the king, because they saw that the wisdom of God was within him, to create justice.

—1 KINGS 3:1, 16–28

IF YOUR HUSBAND EVER offers to buy you peacocks as a wedding present, just say no. In the seven years since I married King Solomon of Israel, I have seen wives, concubines, court officials, prophets, and priests come and go—but the peacocks unfortunately remain. Every morning well before daybreak, those horrible birds not only ruin my rest but wake every one of my maids. Fortunately, my two small children somehow manage to sleep, but still the peacock howls give me headaches. But what can I do, so far from home?

I am Tashere, beloved daughter of Pharaoh Sheshonk I of the twenty-second dynasty of Egypt, living in Jerusalem, given to King Solomon in a political alliance.[1] I no longer ask myself what my life would have been like if I had been allowed to marry my cousin as my mother had planned. No . . . I am here. How my ancestors cry out from their desert tombs, echoing the words of the great Pharaoh Amenhotef III: "From ancient times the daughter of an Egyptian King is given to no one."[2] The daughters of Pharaohs were too important to leave our land. But now this custom is

---

1. Mulder seeks to identify the pharaoh whose daughter married Solomon and suggests, "many interpreters think of Sheshonk I, the founder of the 22nd—or Lybian—dynasty which must have ruled approx. from 946–925 BC and whose name is also found in I Kings 14:25. This Sheshonk or Shishak was the ruler of the city-state Herakleopolis and, as the leader of a group of Lybian soliders, elevated Tanis and Bubastis in the eastern Nile delta to the main seats of the dynasty." Mulder, 1 Kings 1–11, 131–32. Other scholars suggest that biblical chronology points to an earlier pharaoh as the father of Solomon's Egyptian wife, but consensus leans toward Sheshonk.

2. Ibid. Amenhotef is sometimes known by his Greek name, Amenophis.

gone and Israel is a strong country worthy of a marriage alliance. And this is where my children were born so I try to devote myself to this life.

This task is not easy for I still live like a nomad in a tent, perpetually waiting for the palace to be completed. I had heard that people in this region lived in these houses of cloth, but I never thought that I would not only reside in such a dwelling but give birth in one! Oh, mother! Sometimes I am glad you never lived to see your daughter come to this. Here I am, a princess, sitting in quarters that would be for workers in my land, as I gaze at my sons still sleeping, despite the screeching peacocks. It is strange to watch my own children grow up comfortable as Israelites while I still struggle to adjust to this enigmatic land of one god.

I am lost in these thoughts when my peace is interrupted by a servant girl. She peers in the tent, requesting permission to enter, and then delivers a message. I have been summoned by my husband, King Solomon of Israel, to join him on a venture outside of the palace. We are to survey the area where he wants to build an addition to the palace. He knows how hard it is for me here—one of many wives in Israel, but a true princess in Egypt. Egypt is a formidable country and Solomon is political enough to know that treating me well will put him in good favor with the Pharaoh. Solomon and I also get along nicely. I am strong-willed, like him, and I speak my mind with courtesy and clarity.

So I am glad to go. I had told my husband just the day before that surely all this construction would go faster and more efficiently if proper sacrifices were made to Ptah, the architect of worlds.[3] Solomon did not want to hear this and muttered something about idolatry that would be the ruin of him.[4] Yet overall, he is quite understanding of my beliefs. Before the birth of our children, I made an offering to Khnum, who brings fertility

---

3. Allen, *Genesis in Egypt*, 43–44. In this ancient Egyptian creation poem, the God Ptah of Memphis is described at great length as not only creator but architect of the world.
So was made all construction and all craft,
the hands' doing, the feet's going, and every limb's movement,
according as he governs that which the heart thinks,
which emerges through the tongue,
and which facilitates everything.
It has developed that Ptah is called 'He who made all and caused the gods to develop,'
since he is Ta-tenen, who gave birth to the gods,
from whom everything has emerged
food-offerings and sustenance, gods' offerings, and every perfect thing.

4. See 1 Kgs 11:1–10.

and shapes and molds children in the womb.[5] While I know that Solomon was not pleased, he said nothing. Does Solomon actually think that both of our children would have been sons if I had not performed the sacred rites?! He frowned when I suggested this to him. Oh well, if he is going to be so stubborn, I suppose he is going to have to be understanding when his other wives give him daughters.

I have to admit that Solomon is handsome even when he is angry. He is tall and strong with broad shoulders. I love his curly hair, surprisingly fair, and when he laughs, he opens his mouth wide and all his teeth show. I am small with darker skin. My straight hair is as black as night; I have been told it is color of dark wine grapes.[6] Despite having two children, I am still narrow-hipped and slim. In truth we are a good match, my husband and I.

I am grateful that the king is still interested in me with so many other women around to distract him. However, I do worry that I see less and less of him these days. While powerful and kind, he is also fickle and easily distracted. I thank the gods every day that I remain one of his favorites, but who knows how long that will last. He changes women like others change clothes. His minions and officials call this part of his wisdom, but I disagree. I have seen how little it takes for wives and their children to fall out of favor. Entire families get cast out of the royal tents. Wives and children are sent away and forgotten.

That is why I carry my combs with me wherever I go. They are made of the finest ivory and are by far my most valuable material possessions.[7] Not only are they two of the few items that are actually mine, but they also remind me of my home and my mother. These exquisite combs were part of my dowry. They are exactly the size of the palms of my hands, just as they were exactly the size of my mother's palms. Although I favor my father, my hands are identical to my mother's. Sometimes when I am holding the baby, I imagine that my hands are actually hers.

5. Tyldesley, *Daughters of Isis*, 227. According to Tyldesley, Khnum is one of the earliest recorded gods in the Egyptian pantheon who was particularly concerned with the birth of royal children. Khnum is depicted as modeling the body and soul of the infant Hatchepsut, the longest-reigning woman pharaoh, on his celestial potter's wheel.

6. There is a priestess named Mutirdis, depicted in the Louvre C100 stela, who is described as having locks of hair black as night and dark as "wine-grapes," "brilliant" arms, firm breasts and a complexion "like jasper." Green, "Beauty," 168.

7. Ivory combs are among the oldest archeological discoveries in Egypt, some dating back to the pre-dynastic period. Hairstyling was symbolically important, demonstrating social standing, rank, and wealth. Several tomb reliefs depict queens in the afterlife being coiffed by their maids. Watterson, *Women in Ancient Egypt*, 113.

The combs are decorated with the ibis that drinks the waters of the Nile and its tributaries back home in Egypt. There are no birds nearly that graceful here. If anything truly terrible happened, if Solomon dismissed me or war overtook the land, I could sell these combs and take my children with me back to my father's house.

I know that many of the other women must be worried about their futures the way I fret about mine. The court is a dangerous place. Being a favorite wife is challenging and does not make me particularly popular. I tell all of my secrets to my maid, Bilpa. She is the only woman I confide in. Though she is an Israelite, she grew up in Egypt and came with me as part of my dowry. She delivered both my children, and I trust her with my life. I am not close to the other wives or other women at court. They are silly and gossip freely with each other, quickly making personal affairs into public issues. I would never risk the humiliation or Solomon's anger.

Whenever I look at the children Solomon and I have had together, I feel a mixture of pride and fear. Being the oldest sons of Solomon's first wife, they are the most highly honored among all of the children. This also puts them most at risk. I know what often happens to promising young boys, for I have seen such treachery in my own family. Too many of my little playmates disappeared or were sent away when family infighting became too intense! Sometimes I envy common mothers. They may be poor and have to work for food and clothing, but they never worry about their children being poisoned by their sister wives. To protect my sons, I made a special wand out of hippopotamus tusk. I cut it in half and decorated it with the symbols of the hippopotamus-headed goddess, Taweret, and the dwarf god, Bes, and hung it where they sleep. I had it inscribed with a curse that reads: "Cut off the head of the enemy when he enters the chamber of the children whom the lady has borne."[8] Bilpa assures me that my children are safer here than they would be back home in Egypt, but how can I believe her? No sooner do I think about Bilpa than she appears as if conjured. Sometimes I am completely convinced that she is a spirit.

8. The figures of Taweret, the hippopotamus goddess of fertility, and Bes, a dwarf god responsible for the protection of children and the household, were commonly found on wands of this period. "These figures are often associated with apotropaic symbols like the *wedjat* eye, or hieroglyphs like *sa* meaning 'protection,' and *ankh* meaning 'life.' The protective nature of the wand is further made explicit by the inscriptions which some of them bear." Robins, *Women in Ancient Egypt*, 87. The words of the inscription on the wand mentioned above were found in on a wand from the Middle Kingdom. Although this wand is from an earlier time period than when this story is set, similar models likely existed during the 22nd dynasty.

Bilpa helps me to get ready for this outing. First, she slips over my head one of the linen tunics that I had brought from Egypt. The fabric is cool and the streets are so hot and dusty. Why do the people here wear such coarse, unbecoming clothes? Next Bilpa uses my cosmetics palette to apply green eye paint and black eye liner. The other wives make fun of my meticulous makeup and refined garments, but I am not about to give up my personal care habits. My grooming reminds me of my home.

Just as I am dressed, my older son, Sheshonk, wakes up. He is tall like his father but with my teardrop-shaped eyes and straight hair. I named my oldest son after my father and the name suits him well.[9] Like my father, Sheshonk has golden skin and a serious disposition. Yet there is something inquisitive and mischievous in his little face, as if he is just waiting for the right moment to throw a spider at one of the maids or pinch his little brother. He is forever experimenting and making tiny models of buildings. I suppose with all construction going on around him, this should not surprise me. Little Sheshonk begs me to let him follow the workers around and inspect the building material. He tells me in his most grown-up voice that it is his job to make sure they build the palace correctly so it will still be standing when he is king. I pray to the gods that he lives to see such a glorious day. "And I want them to make it extra shiny for my momma!" he adds slyly. His loving desire to please me is mingled with a touch of manipulation. When he learns that I am to go to see a future building site, he pleads with me to allow him to come.

"I could protect you and . . . and . . . and," he stutters and looks at the ground. I am reminded how sweet he is when I look at his little feet kicking the sand. Could I really refuse this child anything?

"Of course you can come, little prince," I reply with a gentle smile.

He looks up, surprised that I gave in without an argument. It will be good for him to go and remind his father how big he is getting. I would love for Solomon to pay more attention to Sheshonk.

With my preparations completed, I hand the baby, Pimay, to Bilpa. Just six months old, Pimay is too little to come with us, but I hate to leave him behind. He has a gentle spirit with the wise eyes of a little old man. He has just learned to sit up. When he smiles, you can see his three new teeth. I warn Bilpa to watch Pimay closely and to keep him far away from Naamah while I am gone. Naamah, the Ammonite, is Solomon's most cunning and devious

9. Mothers name children more frequently than fathers in the Hebrew Bible. See Bohmbach, "Names and Naming," 37.

wife. While she says her name means "agreeable," I think she is about as trust-worthy as a jackal. She will stop at nothing to make sure her son, Rehoboam, is the king's favorite.[10] I even overheard some of the other wives whispering about her involvement in a plot to poison one of the other royal children. I must always remember to be vigilant about the safety of my sons.

Sheshonk and I meet Solomon in front of my tent. Solomon slips an arm around my waist. "I compare you, my love, to a mare among Pharaoh's chariots."[11] He does have a way with words. If only I always had him to myself. He scoops up Sheshonk, who suddenly looks very small in his father's arms.

We climb into the chariot and head off down the streets toward the intended site for the palace addition. I am fearful that a bigger palace will inevitably mean more wives. Suddenly there is a commotion ahead of us. The guards that flank us on either side jump forward to defend the king. I hear women shouting and screaming as Sheshonk burrows close to me and hides his face in the folds of my dress. I instinctively cover his little ears with my hands and wrap myself around him. Out of the chaos, two women push their way forward toward the king, bursting through the crowd. From what they are wearing, loose tunics that slip revealingly, I gather that they must be prostitutes. Both of them are dressed in shades of crimson and wear colorful veils. Their limbs are weighed down with gold ornaments that jangle and glitter in the sun.[12] One of the women is clutching a screaming newborn. The other is forcefully trying to tear the child from the first woman's grip. They throw themselves in front of the king as he dismounts from the chariot. The chaos of the moment subsides as everyone grows hushed, subdued by his regal presence. One of the guards is nursing a bloody nose. Apparently, one of the prostitutes hit him in the face in her attempts to reach the king.

Solomon calls for order as I ask him what he is doing.

He turns around to face me and says quickly but gently, almost in a whisper: "I am the King, my love, and as King I must bring justice to the people." Then he faces the women and speaks loudly with authority. "Stop your quarreling and control yourselves. You, take the baby." The uninjured guard steps forward and takes the screaming infant from the woman, who now has no choice but to let him go. The baby is not comforted and

10. When Solomon dies, Rehoboam, son of Naamah the Ammonite, succeeds him as king. See 1 Kgs 11:43; 14:21.

11. See Song 1:9. Some scholars suggest that the Song of Songs chronicles the love between Pharaoh's daughter and King Solomon.

12. According to biblical texts, prostitutes would cover their faces (Gen 38:15); wear crimson clothes (Jer 4:30); and put on ornaments and eye makeup (Jer 4:30; Ezek 23:40).

continues howling as both women begin talking at once. Each tries to speak more loudly than the other. I can't help but be horrified as the story unfolds.

Apparently, I am correct. The two women are prostitutes, but not cultic sacred prostitutes, for worshipping the gods this way is an abomination in this land. These are ordinary side-of-the-road prostitutes. Here this occupation is not forbidden as long as the women are unmarried.[13] One woman is tall with long black hair; her slender arms shake as her fists clench. The other is short, broad and significantly darker. Her eyes look empty. The tall one speaks first explaining that the two women live together in the same house and both recently gave birth, just three days apart. I look at their hands and notice that their fingernails are caked with dirt. I try to imagine what their house must look like. I think about these two women who surely must have helped each other give birth now fighting in the street like dogs. Then I am shaken from my musing as the tall woman begins to speak again, her voice high pitched and strained from anger. "This woman's son died in the night, because she lay on him!" A gasp escapes my lips and is gone before I can catch it. How terrible to roll over your own baby in the night . . . How could that woman be so careless?

The tall one continues, "So she got up in the middle of the night and took my son from beside me while your servant slept. She laid him at her breast, and she laid her dead son at my breast. When I got up in the morning to nurse my son—he was dead! But when I looked closely at him in the morning, clearly it was not my son that I had borne."

At this point, the small one screams with painful conviction, "No! My son is *alive* and your son is *dead*!"

The tall one tosses her thick head of black curls haughtily. "No! Because *my* son is alive and *your* son is dead!"

I watch in horror as these two women dare to argue with each other before the king.

Solomon raises his hands in a gesture that commands silence. He takes a step back as he assesses the women. Scratching his bearded chin, he eyes them carefully. Their soiled but brightly colored veils flap in the dusty wind. He sighs deeply, then speaks gravely.

"The one says, 'My son is alive and your son is dead.'" He gestures with his chin in the direction of the shorter woman. Then he looks at the taller prostitute: "And that one says, 'No, because your son is dead and my son is

13. Brenner, *Israelite Woman*, 78.

alive."' The king next directs his attention to his head guard and commands, "Bring me a sword."

I feel myself beginning to swoon. Surely, he is not going to have these women publicly executed! They have committed no crime worthy of that. He continues, "Divide the living boy in two; then give half to the one, and half to the other." This is too horrible to bear and I clutch my own living son to my chest. I will not allow my child to witness such brutality. I begin to get out of the chariot to protest when Solomon firmly motions that I am to stay put. How can he expect me to just watch the father of my children cut a baby in half?! Surely the gods will curse him and his house for this grievous offense. But I cannot go against the King and so I stand still . . . thwarted, upset, scared.

Then the short woman steps forward and with a voice full of anguish begs Solomon to let the other woman keep the baby. Her face is streaming with tears. The black kohl that she used to line her eyes drips down her cheeks. She pleads while crying, "Oh, my lord, give her the living boy; certainly do not kill him!" She is sobbing now. The tall one responds coolly, "It shall be neither for me or for you—Divide it!" Solomon looks at me. He then looks at our own child and smiles. How can he go through with this barbarism! Why is he smiling at our son?! What is he thinking?! I can never look at my husband again! I will sell my combs and go back to Egypt. What else can I do? I can't live with a baby killer; what if he should kill our children next? I have enough to worry about with the evil scheming of the other wives. I cannot believe he looks so calm. I feel as if I might be sick right here.

But Solomon does not cut the baby in two. Instead he motions to the guard holding the baby. "Give her the living child," he pronounces, gesturing to the woman pleading for mercy. "Certainly do not kill him. She is his mother." The guard then hands the baby to the small dark woman. Shaking with emotion, she hugs the newborn tightly to her chest. The infant stops screaming. This is the true mother—the one who would rather see her child live with a sworn enemy than be slaughtered like a lamb at the market place. The crowd that had gathered to witness the spectacle now stands and cheers. All of the people are overwhelmed by the king's wisdom. Since many have witnessed this scene, the news of Solomon's justice will travel quickly throughout the land.

As the crowds disperse, I let out a sigh of relief. My husband truly is wise. He walks over and helps me down from the chariot. Sheshonk is shaken but sturdy enough to stand on his own. Taking my hands in his, Solomon looks tenderly into my eyes.

"Are you alright?"

"Fine," I lie. He is unconvinced.

"Beloved," he says, "I owe the wisdom of my judgment to Yahweh in heaven, but also to you here on earth. When I watch you with our sons and see the way you love and protect them, I know what a true mother would do.[14] In order to determine who was the mother of this child, I simply had to imagine you."

As he helps me back into the chariot and we ride off toward the building site, I feel this event slowly sink in. We have not even reached our destination, and this has already been a full day. I wonder what the other wives and maids will say when I tell them about this outing. I still have so much to learn about this surprising man that I call my husband and this strange land with peacocks that is now my home.

Discussion Questions

1. In this story, Tashere is fiercely protective of her sons. Whom or what do you feel compelled to protect? Why?

2. While the story of two women who come to Solomon fighting over a baby is well-known, the biblical specification that the women are prostitutes is not. Why do you think that detail is included? What difference does it make if the women are prostitutes?

3. In the Bible, Solomon's Egyptian wife gets little attention, but in this story she inspires Solomon's famous wisdom. Do you think that women in ancient Israel had more influence than the Bible acknowledges? How could women exercise power? What clues does the text offer about women's influence and agency?

14. The inspiration for this final scene came from an essay by Phyllis Bird on prostitutes in ancient Israel. Bird suggests that the story in 1 Kgs 3:16–28 does not humanize or uphold the prostitutes as women, but stereotypes women as mother. The folkloric nature of this story directly appeals to the audiences' desire to see the woman as "bound by the deepest emotional bonds to the fruit of her womb." Bird, "Harlot as Heroine," 110.

Bibliography

Allen, James P. *Genesis in Egypt: The Philosophy of Ancient Egyptian Creation Accounts.* New Haven: Yale Egyptological Seminar, 1988.

Bird, Phyllis. "The Harlot as Heroine." In *Women in the Hebrew Bible*, edited by Alice Bach, 99–117. New York: Routledge, 1999.

Bohmbach, Karla G. "Names and Naming in the Biblical World." In *Women in Scripture: A Dictionary of Named and Unnamed Women in the Hebrew Bible, the Apocryphal/ Deuterocanonical Books, and the New Testament*, edited by Carol Meyers, Toni Craven, and Ross S. Kraemer, 33–39. Grand Rapids: Eerdmans, 2000.

Brenner, Athalya. *The Israelite Woman: Social Role & Literary Type in Biblical Narrative.* Sheffield, UK: JSOT Press, 1985.

Green, Lyn. "Beauty." In *The Oxford Encyclopedia of Ancient Egypt*, edited by Donald P. Redford, 167–71. Oxford: Oxford University Press, 2005.

Mulder, Martin. *Historical Commentaries on the Old Testament. Volume 1: 1 Kings 1–11.* Leuven: Peeters, 1998.

Robins, Gay. *Women in Ancient Egypt.* Avon: Bath Press, 1993.

Tyldesley, Joyce. *Daughters of Isis: Women of Ancient Egypt.* London: Viking, 1994.

Watterson, Barbara. *Women in Ancient Egypt.* New York: St. Martin Press, 1991.

Vessels of Hope

Julie Faith Parker

1 One woman from the women[1] of the company of the prophets cried to Elisha, "Your servant my husband is dead; and you know that your servant feared Yahweh, but a creditor has come to take my two children for himself as slaves!" *2* Elisha said to her, "What can I do for you? Tell me, what do you have in the house?" She answered, "Your servant has nothing in the entire house, except a cruet of oil." *3* He said, "Go outside, ask for vessels from all your neighbors, empty vessels and not just a few. *4* Then go in and shut the door behind you and your children, and start pouring into all these vessels; then set each aside when it is full."

5 So she left him and shut the door behind her and her children; they kept bringing vessels to her, and she kept pouring. *6* When the vessels were full, she said to her son, "Bring me another vessel." But he said to her, "There are no more vessels." Then the oil stopped flowing.

7 She came and told the man of God, and he said, "Go sell the oil and pay your debts, and you and your children can live on the rest."[2]

—*2 KINGS 4:1–7*

1. The Hebrew word for "woman" or "wife," 'iššâ, appears twice in the beginning of this verse, first in the singular then in the plural. Frequently translated as "wife," the protagonist of this story is no longer a wife since her husband has died. The text never calls her a widow. The phrase "women of the company of the prophets" may suggest that the women married to prophets have their own group.

2. For detailed analysis of this biblical passage, see Parker, *Valuable and Vulnerable*, 119–35.

THE CRUET HAD ALWAYS been precious to me, but little did I expect that it would become an instrument of salvation.

This little jug had been my most prized possession, made by my grandmother and given to me by my mother. The women in my family were potters, known for our jars with remarkably thin clay walls, making them relatively light and easy to carry. My grandmother was not only skilled but talented in crafting her pieces for optimum use. This vessel showed her finest work: a solid base for grounding the small jug securely, a slender bulb that curved up to the mouth with a slight lip for easy pouring, and a handle just big enough to slip two fingers through. We filled this cruet not with basic water, but with oil that would flow out like liquid sun. My mother gave me this vessel, beautiful in its simplicity, when she sent me away to be married. How we held each other and cried, not knowing if we would ever see each other again. Indeed, that was the last day I saw my mother and this cruet was my one treasured link to her.[3]

I remember the words that she whispered in my ear as we were clinging to each other in those final moments: "May the gods grant you sons." Men always told their wives that they needed to bear sons to carry on their line of inheritance and bring honor to the family name, as if women had the power to determine whether the baby was a boy or girl. Women wanted sons too, but for different reasons. Mothers could not bear the pain of parting with daughters. Your sweet girls, the babies who are like you and delight you when they are small and help you more and more as they grow older, become part of your very self. Then the day comes when they get married and move to the home of their husband who might take them far away . . . and a piece of you is gone forever.

In spite of my young age—barely fourteen—when I left my mother, or perhaps because of it, I managed the separation relatively well as I became part of my husband's household.[4] For my mother, my leaving her household

---

3. The Hebrew word for "cruet" in 2 Kgs 4:2 ('āsūk) is a hapax legomenon, meaning this exact word only appears once in the entire Bible. In the context of this essay, this unique word indicates a small vessel of exceptional quality.

4. Life expectancy was much shorter in the ancient world than today, and most people lived 30–40 years. Girls would marry when they began to menstruate, and young men would get married when about ten years older. Ancient Israelite society was patrilocal, with the girl moving into the household of her new husband. This practice also produced a desire for sons, since a family with only daughters would be bereft of offspring to care for aging parents. For details on marriage in the ancient Near East, see Marsman, *Women in Ugarit and Israel*, 84–106. For a review of biblical texts related to marriage, see Yamauchi, "Marriage," 221–26.

was pure loss, but for me there was a new life to create. My father, who loved me dearly, thought he was doing the best he could for me in arranging my marriage, and for a while it seemed he was right. In the years just before I left my father's house, the harvests had been so sparse. The vessels that the women in my family made and sold kept us alive. My mother would bring two clay jars to a neighbor's home. One she would leave there, and the other she would bring back full of grain, figs, or oil—whatever the neighbor might have. We always managed to have enough to eat, but just barely. My father thought that if I married someone who did not toil to earn a meager living from the ground, I might not know hunger. So he married me to a prophet.

My husband, Obad,[5] was kind, and for that I was so grateful. He was older than I was, but only by about five years, younger than most men who marry. Yet ever since he was a child, Obad had an undeniable gift for healing. People with milky white eyes, so clouded that they appeared to have no eyes at all, would travel great distances—often days on end—to get to Obad. He would gently place his hands on their faces, say a prayer to the gods, and the whiteness would disappear.[6] The miracle of vision filled the healed ones with generous gratitude; they gave him grain or cloth or oil or pots . . . sometimes even spices or wine. Word of such power travels fast, and Obad had goods beyond his years, making him eligible for marriage. His powerful reputation was attractive, and I believed my father when he told me that I would not have to worry about survival with Obad at my side. As I said, I was young, and obviously naïve.

The gods looked favorably upon us at first and our early years together passed peacefully. I bore Obad a son and a daughter. I was relieved that our first child, Oseh, was a boy; I had fulfilled my duty as a wife. Our gentle boy was like his father. Both had strong builds, straight brown hair, and dark eyes that always appeared to be absorbed in thought. A second child, shortly after Oseh, never made its way into the world. I know the moment that caused me to miscarry: just one drink of water from the spring near Jericho and my stomach started to convulse.[7] That baby was gone, but a little over a year later it was replaced in my heart by our daughter, Amayah. I remembered my

5. The ancient historian Josephus designated the woman in this passage as the wife of Obadiah (*Antiquities* 9.4.2).

6. References to being blind, likely caused by trachoma, appear nearly 100 times in the Bible. See King and Stager, *Life in Biblical Israel*, 75.

7. See 2 Kgs 2:18–22.

mother's words when she was born. I knew that I should be disappointed, but how I could not rejoice when our daughter came into the world healthy and strong? Like me, she had soft, thick, dark hair. She grew into a girl who melted everyone's heart with her musical laugh and gift for finding joy.

But gifts are not like skills. Skills can be learned. You can acquire and control your skills. Gifts can be forgotten, lost, ruined, or destroyed. And gifts come from the gods, over whom we have no control. They can be mercurial and snatch their favors away as quickly as they bestow them. And so it happened with Obad.

As before, the blind continued to come to him, groping their way along hot and stony roads, the lucky ones with a family member or two who could be spared to make the trip. These struggling travelers bore burdens of treasures to bestow upon my husband, in payment for his healing.[8] Yet one man who came to him, we don't know who, apparently got sick again after Obad had healed him, and his blindness returned. He started spreading rumors that Obad had left him blind, even after payment. It wasn't true! But lies can grow into false truths that take on their own demonic life.

People stopped coming . . . and so there was no payment. Even worse, for the few who did come, Obad's gifts were clearly fading. When a blind person was approaching our home, I could see the doubt on my husband's face. When the blind person stood before him, Obad would place his fingers on the supplicant's clouded eyes, as he had done hundreds of times before, but now no change took place. As grateful and joyous as the healed once had been, those who remained without sight felt cheated and angry. Why had they come all this way for nothing?! Obad would try again and again—highlighting his inabilities—and all to no avail. Sharing their heartbreak, my husband would apologize profusely. No one felt worse than he did. I also felt terrible and we would invite the travelers to stay with us for a few days to restore their strength before the journey home. This hospitality rapidly drained our food supplies, but sharing this kindness lessened the guilt and the sorrow that we felt.

Yet it increased the worry.

Why had Obad's healing gifts left him? It was as if the gods believed the lie too. Perhaps some of the gods wanted to see us suffer; they can be jealous, even of mortals, and our life had been so good. We needed a god who would help us, and perhaps even stand up to the other gods and give Obad his gift

---

8. Multiple texts suggest that prophets were paid for their services. See 1 Sam 9:6–8; 1 Kgs 14:1–3; 2 Kgs 5:3–5, 20–23; Amos 7:12.

back. About this time, we started to hear about a new deity—the curious god who had no statue, with the strange name of Yahweh. Perhaps he had taken away Obad's abilities because we had not sacrificed to him?

This god was clearly gaining power where we lived in the hill country of Ephraim; one of his prophets was even organizing groups of followers. We heard that this prophet was a bald man who angered easily, but whose powers were extraordinary. Wild stories were circulating about all the wonders he could perform, far beyond the usual healing of blindness or crooked limbs. People claimed that he saw horses of fire, and could control fierce beasts.[9] They said he made an ax head float and could even bring someone back from the dead![10] It was hard to know what to believe. However, many people from Jericho had witnessed him curing the foul spring that had made me miscarry, so we reasoned that there must be *some* truth to all of these stories. Perhaps this prophet, named Elisha, could help Obad get his gift back.

And so when Elisha came through our region asking who wanted to be part of his company of prophets, Obad was quick to volunteer. Other prophets whom Elisha had gathered also clustered in our village, bringing their families.[11] The members of this company of prophets were to live together, perform their works of wonder, and give credit to the god Yahweh. They would also do the bidding of Elisha.

Obad and I welcomed the other prophets and their families to the hill country. Although our living became crowded with so many people clustered together, I loved this new situation. Since our husbands traveled together to perform their works of healing, we wives formed our own group and called ourselves "the women of the company of the prophets."[12] With our husbands away so often we quickly became a close and caring community. I taught the women and their daughters how to make vessels, as my mother had taught me. Our work was hard as we maintained our households and shared whatever our husbands received for their acts of healing. While we women worked, we talked and laughed and shared in the raising of our children. As our husbands made the sick become healthy, we

---

9. See 2 Kgs 2:11–25.

10. See 2 Kgs 6:1–7 and 2 Kgs 4:8–37. The collection of stories about Elisha's works of wonder appear primarily in 2 Kgs 1–8, in no particular order. One tale is not contingent on another.

11. Robert Wilson notes that the company of the prophets was a group that apparently lived in community. Wilson, *Prophecy and Society*, 202.

12. This phrase appears in 2 Kgs 4:1.

wives turned grain into bread, wool into tunics, clay into vessels, and food into babies through the wonders of our pregnancies. Our miracles were not prophetic gifts, but the everyday kind that took the abilities of our bodies and the knowledge of our hands. Our husbands relied on us as we relied on them. Amidst kind people and meaningful work, Oseh and Amayah were growing strong. Our lives would have been wonderful, if I hadn't been so worried about Obad.

Even in the company of the prophets, it seemed that my husband's gifts did not return. He became very devoted to Yahweh, praying multiple times a day and making sacrifices, but for some reason, Yahweh did not show favor to him. Maybe Yahweh was jealous of Obad's earlier success, as the other gods had been. Obad was kinder than Elisha; perhaps Yahweh was worried that Obad would overshadow his chosen prophet. Regardless, my husband was struggling to find his lost gift and to keep his failures a secret.

Obad could see that our children were thriving and that I was so happy; I knew he would do anything for us—but I so wish he had not acted as he did. In the morning, the company of the prophets would assemble and decide where they would go. When Elisha was with us, he would give orders as to exactly what the company should do, but usually he was some-place else and the prophets would decide for themselves. They would select a town, walk there, and perform healings along the way and then among the townspeople, bringing back what they had been paid. Obad would set out with the others, but he would come home on his own, apparently diverging from the group. I asked him why, and he told me that his pow-ers worked best when he was alone. Because he brought back such fine payment, I believed him, although I should have questioned him more. The goods Obad obtained were of far better quality than those of the other prophets. They returned with sacks of grain or wool for spinning. Obad re-turned with pomegranates, dates, and honey, cloth already woven, and even striped cloth! He said that Yahweh told him who needed healing and could pay the highest price, for the good of the group. Since all of the prophets shared what they earned, the other prophets were not jealous; everyone was glad for Obad's success. The men and the women of the company of the prophets regarded him, and therefore me as well, with great respect. I was so content that I foolishly let myself believe that what Obad said was true, even though, deep down, I knew better.

I could tell from Obad's eyes that he was troubled. If I had just pressed him harder for the truth! I discovered all that had happened the day that

Obad's dead body was dragged to my door. The money lender brought him and explained that I could have the body, but that he would be taking Obad's tunic as soon as I removed it from my dead husband. Shock, sadness, and fear filled my soul and poured out in an anguished cry. "Nooooo . . . my beloved Obad!" I held his bruised and bloodied body as the creditor stared at me impatiently. Oseh and Amayah ran to my side and started sobbing too, once they saw their father's body.

The women of the company of the prophets quickly surrounded me. As I wailed on the floor, rocking back and forth next to my lifeless husband, some of the women hugged Oseh and Amayah, holding them firmly and gently. Some comforted me, rocking alongside me, sharing my tears, rubbing my back. And some were like attack dogs on the creditor. With strength in numbers, the women forced him to leave Obad's dead body and our cluster of homes. He angrily stormed off and I heard him yell, with cruelty in his voice, that he would be back to collect what he was owed.

As word of Obad's death spread, we came to learn what had happened. Obad had hoped that Yahweh would restore his gifts, but this jealous god never did. Instead, desperately wanting to contribute to the company of the prophets, Obad would go to the creditor seeking goods. He promised to return payment as soon as he was able, believing that Yahweh would eventually reward his faithfulness and restore his powers so he would once again have plenty of resources. Yet the creditor had lured Obad into terrible debt by providing items far more luxurious than Obad had requested, while promising that Obad could pay him back whenever his powers returned. Then one day, the creditor had had enough and suddenly turned on him. When Obad came to him for more goods, the creditor began screaming, chasing after Obad as he fled. When he caught up to Obad, the creditor pushed my husband off a steep path into a deep ravine, sending him to his death. The creditor would not admit to this, but travelers on the road had heard Obad's screams and saw the creditor staring with satisfaction at Obad's body below. And then this creditor had the nerve to drag the lifeless body to me as proof of the money owed him.

How could I possibly pay back all that was owed for such beautiful things? With more time, I could make vessels, but clay was hard to find in these hills and it took time to make vessels properly. When the creditor came again, I was alone in the house with my children; most of the women were attending to a young woman who was giving birth. I believe the creditor was a little afraid of all the women, so he waited until they were away. I had stayed at the house to make vessels, as many and as quickly as I could, anticipating this dreaded moment.

"Your husband owed me for many fine goods. How can you pay?" This was the voice I heard when I looked up from my work to see beady eyes bearing down on me. I stood up to gain some height; the children scurried to my side.

"I have many items here in my household and I am making vessels," I told him, working hard to keep my voice calm. "I will sell them and pay you what we owe."

"Yes, I will take all of this," he said, clearly unimpressed as he looked around our dwelling. "But that is not nearly enough to pay me for all that I gave your husband." Then he turned his gaze to the children—Oseh, now twelve years old, and Amayah, just ten. "They look like strong workers." The way he stared at Amayeh made me sick to my stomach. "I can take them as my slaves."[13]

"You. Will. *Not!*" I screamed at him, punctuating each word.

He was startled by my fierce response, unused to such talk from a woman. But I had been strengthened by the women of the company of the prophets.

"I will take what you have for now," the creditor said, regaining his control. "Yet I will be back soon."

Just a short way from the house, I saw a boy about Oseh's age. The starving child's face was full of fear; it was the look of someone mercilessly beaten. The creditor sent the boy to take things from our house, which he did. Not wanting to stand there while this sad child gathered our possessions, I grabbed the cruet that my mother had given me, hid it in my tunic, and ran out with my children to find the other women. There was only one way that I could keep my precious Oseh and Amayah: I needed a miracle.

The women of the company of the prophets came up with a plan. They told me that I should appeal to Elisha the next time he came to our area. His powers were far greater than those in the company of the prophets; he would find a way to pay the creditor. But the creditor would be back soon, and when would Elisha come? How could I know?

Perhaps Yahweh was taking pity on me and regretted not giving Obad his powers back, because when the creditor came the next time, Elisha did

---

13. Debt slavery was common in the ancient Near East. See Chirichigno, *Debt-Slavery*, 30–144. Children would be valued as slaves because they were easier to control than adults and cost less to feed.

too. A few days later the creditor appeared at my house and told me that he had sold all my goods but that was not enough to cover the debt. "But I will not kill you," he offered, as if this were a kindness. "I have only come to take your two children to serve me." Again, he looked at Amayah intently.

I dashed out past him, holding each child by the hand. The creditor followed me, but the women of the company of the prophets stopped him while I ran and found Elisha speaking with the men. I knew that I should not speak so directly with a man so powerful, but I was desperate. As soon as I saw Elisha, I cried out, "Your servant my husband is dead; and you know that your servant feared Yahweh, but a creditor has come to take my two children for himself as slaves!"

I think that the prophets had been telling Elisha about my dire predicament, because he was quick to respond. As if coming up with a plan, Elisha immediately asked me, "What can I do for you? Tell me, what do you have in the house?"

I told him the truth: "Your servant has nothing in the entire house, except a cruet of oil."

Yahweh must have given him insight, or perhaps the prophets had told him about all the vessels I was making. Elisha knew that my neighbors would have containers. He instructed me, "Go outside, ask for vessels from all your neighbors, empty vessels and not just a few. Then go in and shut the door behind you and your children, and start pouring into all these vessels; then set each aside when it is full."

I immediately did as the prophet had said, closing the door to the house so the creditor could not see what was happening inside. I sent Oseh and Amayah to get vessels from all our neighbors; they ran and lugged jars into the house as quickly as they could. I poured oil from my mother's cruet into all the vessels. The oil kept pouring! It was the miracle that I had hoped for! When all the vessels in the house were full, I asked Oseh for another vessel and he told me that there were no more. Then the oil stopped flowing.

I opened the door, went out of the house, and saw Elisha standing there. I told him that the vessels were now all filled with oil. Elisha smiled. "Go sell the oil and pay your debts, and you and your children can live on the rest."

The oil was of far better quality than any I had ever seen. I would have enough money to pay all the debts and sustain our family for a long time.

I was overjoyed! I could keep my children!!

I had heard that Yahweh cared about those who suffered, but until now I had not believed it. The power of this god—combined with the power a prophet and the power of a community of women—had saved my children from the bitter life of slaves. Like my cruet, these women, this prophet, and this god had become my vessels of hope.

Discussion Questions

1. As with many miracle stories in the Bible, Elisha's multiplying the woman's supply of oil defies logic. Do you find such stories credible? Why or why not? Have you ever witnessed or experienced a healing or some other occurrence that did not seem entirely logical?

2. Even when she has to give up everything else, the narrator in this story holds onto the cruet that links her to her mother. Do you have any item that is of special significance to you? If so, what it is and why does it matter so much?

3. This story emphasizes the role of community in saving one family from an awful fate. Have you or your family ever been helped by a community during a difficult time? Have you been part of a community that helped someone else?

Bibliography

Chirichigno, Gregory C. *Debt-Slavery in Israel and the Ancient Near East.* Journal for the Study of the Old Testament: Supplementary Series 141. Sheffield: Sheffield Academic Press, 1993.

King, Philip J. and Lawrence W. Stager. *Life in Biblical Israel.* Louisville, Ky.: Westminster John Knox, 2001.

Marsman, Hennie J. *Women in Ugarit and Israel: Their Social and Religious Position in the Context of the Ancient Near East. Oudtestamentische Studiën* 49. Leiden: Brill, 2003.

Parker, Julie Faith. *Valuable and Vulnerable: Children in the Hebrew Bible, Especially the Elisha Cycle.* Brown Judaic Studies Series 355. Providence, R.I.: Brown University, 2013.

Whiston, William, trans. *The Works of Josephus.* Peabody, Mass: Hendrickson, 1987.

Wilson, Robert R. *Prophecy and Society in Ancient Israel.* Philadelphia: Fortress, 1984.

Yamauchi, Edwin M. "Marriage." In *Dictionary of Daily Life in Biblical and Post-Biblical Antiquity,* edited by Edwin M. Yamauchi and Marvin R. Wilson, 221–49. Vol 3. Peabody, Mass.: Hendrickson, 2016.

Appeasing the Death-Loving God

Richard P. Poirier

They have built high places of the Topheth, which is in the Valley of the
Son of Hinnom, to burn their sons and their daughters in the fire—
which I did not command and it did not arise in my heart.

—*JEREMIAH 7:31*

They built the high places of Baal, which are in the valley of the Son of
Hinnom, to offer their sons and their daughters to Molech, which I did
not command them nor did it arise in my heart to do this abomination
to cause Judah to sin.[1]

—*JEREMIAH 32:35*

THE DAY WAS YOUNG and already the heat was blistering. It was the
middle of the wet season, when the rains should have fallen to soften
the ground. But the powerful sun was relentless, and had been this way for
months. People were getting scared. How would we survive without water

---

1. The practice of sacrificing children to gods appears repeatedly in the Hebrew Bible
(e.g., Gen 22:1–14; Deut 12:31; Judg 11:29–40; 2 Kgs 3:26–27; 17:31; Ezek 16:20–21; Ps
106:37–38). Child sacrifice was probably not common among Yahweh worshippers and
some scholars debate whether this practice transpired at all. Nonetheless, certain biblical
texts such as Jer 7:31; 32:35 (above), support the view that child sacrifice took place at the
Topheth in ancient Israel (see also 2 Kgs 23:10). Many scholars understand the Topheth
to be a place in the Hinnom Valley, not too far from Jerusalem, where people would burn
their children as a sacrifice to the god Molech. Sweeney, "Topheth," 1059.

or food? Although the sky looked the same as it had on many other days, this sweltering morning my father had a different expression. It wasn't the uncomfortable worry that I had grown used to, but a deeper look of fear and dread. At first I barely even noticed.

As usual, I woke my older brother and clambered down the ladder from the rooftop where we slept.[2] At least the nights were cool. We pulled some bread from the large jar in the small storeroom to eat before heading to the fields. Our father was standing next to the jar with a vacant look. His eyes never met ours, even when I handed him a piece of bread. That was unusual. Even stranger, he ate barely anything, although we were all becoming increasingly hungry as the food became increasingly sparse. Still, I thought little of it. Perhaps my father was sick or maybe another one of the goats had died. I was simply a boy of twelve, getting ready for another challenging day of trying to coax grain from dry earth.[3]

As we headed toward our family lands, I assumed the day would continue like so many before, little suspecting the horror that lay ahead. My brother, Reuben, my elder by two years, was my father's firstborn, and set to take over as head of the family,[4] but I was always quick to remind him that we were equal in the fields. As soon as we had grown big enough to guide an ox, my brother and I would take turns plowing. One of us would push the plow, guiding the ox forward, and the other would follow, scattering seed. This day we followed the same routine, but it seemed so futile. Why were we wasting seed on dusty earth? Did my father know that rains were coming? Had he consulted with a prophet and heard from the gods? I would have asked him, but his serious face silently told me to stay quiet. So my brother and I did our

2. Houses in ancient Israel commonly had a floor plan with four rooms, or a variation thereof. Three long rooms ran parallel to each other and a fourth horizontal room in the back was used for storage. Archaeologists surmise that homes were generally two stories, based on the amount of debris found in the remains. When the weather allowed, people likely slept on the flat roof of the house, where it was cooler and quieter than inside. For more detailed discussion about Israelite houses, see Borowski, *Daily Life*, 16–21.

3. Children would contribute to the family labor as soon as they were able. Girls generally acquired skills that required technological knowledge, including grinding grain, making bread, weaving cloth, making pottery and caring for children. Boys would acquire skills that required upper body strength, including plowing and harvesting. For discussion of the labor performed by members of the household, see Meyers, *Discovering Eve*, 139–49.

4. Typical family size (with one wife) would average between two and four children who would survive to adulthood. Stager, "Archaeology of the Family," 18. According to Deut 21:17, the oldest son had special status and was entitled to a double portion of the family inheritance. King and Stager, *Life in Biblical Israel*, 37.

work as if it were any other year—hoping, like everyone else, that the heavens would share their moisture. We talked and sang rhythmic songs to make the work go faster; eventually, the sun began to lower toward the land and we headed back to the house for the evening meal.

I was famished (as always) and raced my brother to be the first one home. When we arrived, there was no food prepared for us.

Shocked and disappointed, I ran outside yelling, "Where is the food . . .?!"

I quickly shut my mouth when I saw the elder members of our family clan circled around my father.

Then my father spoke. "Go inside. We will eat when we are done discussing some matters."

I did as I was told. My father's youngest sister, Mara, was inside grinding a few small handfuls of grain. Was this all we had left? She was part of our household, more like a sister than an aunt, for we had grown up together. But she would be married within a year or two and then she would leave us.[5] I sat with Mara, and Reuben soon arrived and joined us. We waited together . . . for what . . . only the gods knew.

I was beginning to grow restless. Perhaps it was the hunger pains in my stomach, but I could not understand what could be so critical that it could not wait until after we had eaten something . . . anything.

Finally I asked my brother, "What's going on? Are we being punished for some unknown sin?"

"Maybe the food stores have grown so meager that they are deciding who gets to eat," he quietly answered. I couldn't believe it; as long as I had been alive, we had always had at least a little grain to put in our stomachs.

Mara spoke up. "I overheard the women talking today while we were gathering fuel for the fire. They said the gods were displeased and punishing us."

"For what?" I asked, genuinely curious.

"Who knows?" she retorted. "They don't tell us. But something must be very wrong for them to keep the windows of the heavens closed."[6]

"Well, then the men must be deciding to make an offering to the gods" I said. "Maybe one of the few remaining goats. Or perhaps they are

5. Family structure in ancient Israel was kinship-based, with related families living together in clustered villages. The society was also patrilocal and a girl would go live with her husband's family upon marriage. See Marsman, *Women in Ugarit and Israel*, 84.

6. Ancients believed that the waters of the skies were sealed off by a dome and the gods opened the windows to let the water pour down (see Gen 7:11–12, 8:2).

planning a trip to one of the shrines or the temple in Jerusalem." My brother nodded in agreement.

Mara paused, then said quietly, "They are talking about sacrifice, but not the kind you have in mind."

"What kind of sacrifice?" my brother asked. "A drink? Grain? An unblemished goat is the best we can offer!"

"What other kind of sacrifice is there?" I asked, exasperated.

Another long pause.

Mara's voice was low. "Reuel, did you know your father and I had an older brother?" I was shocked. What was she talking about? Reuben shared my confusion and jumped in to explain what he knew.

"Our father was his father's eldest son; that is why we live on this plot of land. I am my father's firstborn and one day it will be mine." I rolled my eyes at Reuben. Once again he was reminding me of his status. But I agreed that Mara wasn't making any sense.

She went on: "Your father got the land because of what happened to our older brother."

"What happened to him?" I demanded. Her tone of voice was making me uneasy. Mara collected herself for a moment; what she wanted to say would not come easily.

Slowly she explained. "There was another long drought, much like the one we are experiencing now, when your father was not much older than you. The gods sent scorching heat that spanned three harvest festivals. No manner of animal sacrifice would appease the gods' anger, so the elders agreed that a more powerful offering was needed."

A more powerful offering . . . what could she mean by that?

"What was this offering?" I asked, genuinely bewildered.

"Our older brother was sacrificed to Molech in the Hinnom Valley.[7] Your father was so upset about the death of his brother that he never spoke of him again. I wasn't even born when it happened. I only found out years later from our mother, who told me just before she died. She told me not to speak of him either. That is why you didn't know of his existence."

---

7. Scholars debate whether the word Molech (Hebrew: *mlk*) indicates a type of sacrifice or the name of a Canaanite god who required sacrifice. This essay adopts the latter view, supported by John Day (among others). Day argues that the word *mlk* could not indicate a type of sacrifice because Lev 20:5 describes those who "go whoring after Molech," meaning to follow this god. To understand *mlk* as indicating a type of sacrifice makes no sense in this context. See Day, *Molech*, 11.

I felt as though I had been hit across the face. I stared at the ground for a minute, searching for words. "Did this human sacrifice appease the gods? Did it bring an end to the drought?" My voice was barely audible. I was afraid of the answer.

And Mara was afraid to tell me. She whispered, "Yes."

Now my words came out in a torrent. "So they are planning on doing this again? But that would mean . . .".

Reuben spoke. "I am to be sacrificed."

My brother raised his eyes and looked directly into mine. Aside from our gaze, it felt as if nothing else existed in the world. Then we both broke into tears.

I do not know how long I sat there staring at my brother, losing myself to my emotions. It felt like a bad dream, until my father walked into the house and called for my brother to come outside with him. When my father looked at me, he must have noticed I had been crying.

"Has something happened, Reuel?" he asked gently.

My voice had an edge that I didn't recognize. "Why are you calling Reuben outside?"

Suddenly, he was terse. "We have some things to discuss privately."

I just had to know if it was true. "You're going to sacrifice him, aren't you?"

My father looked stunned. "What did you say?" The words barely escaped his mouth.

"You're going to sacrifice him to pay for whatever we did to bring about the drought."

He nodded slowly and sadly. "Yes, the sacrifice must be paid. We cannot survive like this for much longer. Whatever our family has done, it has been terribly severe. The gods must release the waters or we will all die."

I jumped to my feet as much angry as sad. I felt like a man, ready to challenge my father.

"You can't do this! He is meant to take over your place and lead our family!" Then I crumbled into tears, pleading, "He is my only brother . . .". My father put his hand on my shoulder, and I knew that he was deeply grieved.

"Someday you will understand, my son," he said. And with that, he left the house.

Now I didn't care about food. Maybe if we could all get by without eating, Reuben wouldn't have to die. At some point, I must have lain down on my mat. I do not remember falling asleep; all I remember is drifting in and out of consciousness with an image of my brother looming nearby. Was there anything else we could do to get the gods to give us water? My tears began to flow. Was this really going to happen? When? Where? I had so many questions and no way of knowing the answers.

I awoke with the rising sun, as I did every day. This day looked the same as the previous ones, but felt to me unlike any other. More than the sun bearing down as usual, it now felt as though large stones were crushing my chest. It seemed like a struggle to move, but I eventually got up and went to the storage jar for a morsel of food. My brother was there, waiting for me to go to the fields. No words were spoken between us, and we tried to act as if it were just another day. We did our work in the fields, but today there was no singing. Instead, I silently wondered why the gods were so cruel. Which god was demanding this? I thought of the gods and their powers: Baal, the master of storms; Asherah, the mother goddess; Astarte, the queen of the stars; Yahweh, the jealous god of Abraham; Molech, the fierce god of death.[8] I had known their names as long as I'd known my own; their stone likenesses dwelt in our house. We tried to serve them and we would pour out some of our food to share it with them.[9] We also sent someone from the family to Jerusalem to sacrifice to Yahweh each year. This god seemed to be gaining strength and we did not want to anger him. Had we not done enough? What else did they expect from us? Why did they want to take my brother from me? I hadn't done anything wrong! Then it hit me. In questioning the gods . . . could I be displeasing them and making things worse? The elders would tell us stories of the gods and the wonderful, terrible things they did. They were not like us; they saw everything and became incensed very easily. Then I suddenly realized what I had to do. I could not doubt these powerful gods. I had to accept the sacrifice of my brother otherwise I would make them angrier.[10] If I could stay silent maybe they would relent and give us rain.

8. All of these deities are mentioned in the Bible. The name Baal appears about 90 times, sometimes simply meaning "lord" and other times representing a Canaanite god of storms. The word Asherah appears approximately 40 times, signifying a Canaanite goddess or her symbol of cultic devotion. Astarte is a celestial goddess named nine times. Molech is mentioned eight times, frequently associated with child sacrifice. Repeatedly in the Hebrew Bible, Yahweh, the god of the Israelites, competes with these other deities for dominance. For more detailed discussion about these gods and goddesses, see the entries (by the deity's name) in van der Toorn, *DDD*.

9. Archaeological sites suggest that many religious practices were centered in the home or local shrines until the late eighth century BCE. See Borowski, *Daily Life*, 24–25.

10. Bruce Chilton asserts, "War, famine, and plague could kill so great a proportion

When we walked back from the fields after another hard day, I looked at my brother. I felt helpless. I wished for nothing more than to eat the evening meal and return to the way things had been, but yesterday was now a world away. When we got to the house, I heard my father announce, "Everyone is to gather outside in front of the house." When the extended family had assembled, my father addressed us.

"As you know, we have not had rain for many, many moons. I have consulted my brothers from the neighboring lands, as well as the elders here; the gods surely are displeased. Our animal sacrifices have done nothing to stop the wrath of the gods. So as my father did before me, I will travel with my brother and my two sons to the Hinnom Valley to win back favor for our family. The gods demand the blood of the firstborn child, the most perfect of offerings. I have spoken to Reuben and he knows what he must do. It has been decided—we leave at the turn of the next full moon. I do this with a heavy heart, but the protection of our clan is more important than any one person. If it were possible, I would lay down my life in place of the boy's, but only the blood of a firstborn will suffice, and none of us here can claim that status except Reuben. I will hear no more on this matter."

The group dispersed as quickly as it had gathered. It seemed that everyone had known the news already, even though this was the first public discussion. I then realized that my father had been like me—the brother going off to sacrifice his brother. How did he manage to watch his brother die? How would I?

The next few weeks were agonizingly slow. Sometimes, in a few moments of precious relief, I would forget about my brother's fate—but then as quickly as the thought left me, it would come back hard. I was sad to lose my brother, angry at the gods for demanding him, and afraid that they would know my thoughts and punish us more. There was nothing to do except try to go on. My brother knew it too. His competitive playful self started to fade away, replaced by a shell of the boy-man he had been.

↬

The time had come. My father and his brother, along with my brother and me, loaded up a donkey and began our journey to the Hinnom Valley, in hopes of appeasing the gods. This was my first time to leave the village, and my eyes and ears took in every sight and sound as we traveled over the

---

of the community that people who engaged in sacrifice came to believe the gods enjoyed human victims." Chilton, *Abraham's Curse*, 28.

foreign terrain. It was hot, and I felt the perspiration drip from my brow as I looked up into the blinding sun. I watched a pair of birds high in the sky circling over the corpse of an unfortunate animal that must have wandered too far in this desert. I hoped that we would not share the same fate. We walked all day and my feet grew as heavy as stones, but I did not complain, for fear of angering my father or uncle, who seemed to have no problem with the journey. My focus remained on keeping up with the donkey, whose slow pace gave me hope that I was not falling behind.

The next day was much like the first. We walked up and down hills in the scorching heat of the sun. By midday, fatigue had set in again and my vision became blurry. I stopped to steady myself, but the world around me continued to move. My father must have noticed my difficulties because he fell back to walk at my side. He gave me his arm as support so I could continue. I kept my gaze focused on the donkey as I always had, until my father's voice broke my concentration.

As if reading my mind, my father said, "This is our only option, my son. My father had to make the same decision before me. The tradition can be traced all the way back to the great Abraham, whose god Yahweh, whom we also serve, commanded his son to be offered."[11]

I remembered the story. "But Yahweh spared Abraham's son! Why can't Reuben also be spared?"

My father's tone was sharp and clear, "No. There is no other way. We are sinful men, and cannot measure up to Abraham. Besides, Abraham served only Yahweh, whereas we serve many gods. Some of our gods are not as forgiving as Yahweh."

My father continued, "Fortunately this offering is only required in the most bleak of circumstances. Pray that the gods will find favor with you as they did my grandfather and not demand your son as a sacrifice." For the first time, emotion cracked his voice. "My father and I were weak men and not so fortunate." Attempting to regain himself, my father pointed to a ridge in the distance. "The Hinnom Valley is just over there. The time is nearing . . ." his voice trailed off; I knew he was struggling for composure. He tried to bring some conviction to his tone and added, "When we go this way again on the way home, we will return with the blessing of the gods."

I couldn't help turning my head to look at my brother, who gave me a slow, sad nod. If another traveler had passed us, he would have never guessed that my brother was hours from death. He appeared eerily calm,

11. See Gen 22:1–19.

but I knew him well. His expression was hollow. I tried to draw strength from my brother, but sadness overwhelmed me and I fell back to my position alongside the donkey. I wanted it all to be over. I dared to hope that Yahweh might send *us* an angel too.

When we arrived at the Hinnom Valley, a chill went down my spine. Looking down on this large fissure in the land, I saw an abyss, as dark as death, punctured by jagged rocks that thrust upward out of the ground. My father led us to a pass that would take us down into the valley, but the unwelcoming terrain greeted us with shifting rock and gravel that could send any careless traveler into the pit. When we finally reached the bottom of the valley, I heard my brother mutter: "What kind of a god lives in a place like this?"

I thought, "The kind that desires human blood"—but I said nothing. This was the home of Molech.[12] His name filled me with loathing, made stronger by this foreboding place.

Our first task was to gather enough dry wood to build a large pyre. As much as I hated the task, I couldn't help but think how much worse it must be for my brother, gathering the fuel for his own destruction. It took us until near sundown, but by then we had built a pyre sufficient to produce a flame large enough for a tall boy. Once the physical labor was complete, we sat down to have one final meal together, unwrapping some of the provisions we had brought for the journey. It would be the last time father was to eat with son, brother with brother, uncle with nephew. My father uttered thanks to the gods, then we ate our somber meal in silence. Beyond the glow of the fire reflecting on our faces, all else disappeared into the black shroud of the abyss, producing the ominous sense that we were alone in this world. I kept repeating to myself the words my father had said to me on our journey: "We are men and we have a duty to do." We are men, true, but does that mean we cannot express our anguish? I just tried to retain my composure.

The meal finished and the preparations for the sacrifice began. My father began to wash my brother, and my uncle lit some incense. I wondered how any amount of purification could cleanse such a vile act. When my father began to pour the oil on my brother, I knew that the moment that I had dreaded for so long was at hand. I turned away for fear that my crying, my weakness, might interfere with the ritual in some way. I heard my father and uncle reciting the prayers to Molech. The sharp scent of incense stung my nostrils, and I could feel the heat from the fire, my body welcoming its

12. In Isa 57:9, Molech is associated with Sheol, the underworld.

warmth in the cold of the night. It angered me to think I could find pleasure in any part of this horrific process. The only sound was the crackling fire. It was all I could do to keep myself from sobbing uncontrollably, so I just stared at the ground repeating to myself, "We must appease the gods. We must save the family. We must appease the gods. We must save the family." My thoughts were interrupted by my brother's voice.

"Reuel." Reuben stood before me, his face shining from the oil. "I must leave you, but know that I love you. I give my life for our family. Don't ever forget me, my brother." My throat was closed and my eyes were clouded with tears. All I could manage was a nod. Then I embraced my brother and ran away. I didn't care what my father thought—I couldn't bear to watch Reuben pass through the fire.[13] When I was a long bowshot away, I sat down and cried loudly with my hands over my ears so I wouldn't have to hear the sound of his body burning.

I cried myself into utter exhaustion, then fell asleep on the ground, still a distance from the fire. When I awoke, I looked around this awful valley and realized that the nightmare had been real. I started to cry again, but this time the tears were of sadness . . . and relief. My brother had sacrificed himself for us. A sacrifice so precious *must* appease this death-loving god. Now the worst was over. I got up and walked over to the camp where my father and uncle were still sleeping.

We had done what we needed to do, and I knew that better days lay ahead.

Discussion Questions

1. Many Bible readers familiar with the story of Abraham's sacrifice of Isaac in Genesis 22 do not realize that references to child sacrifice appear in multiple texts. Were you aware that the Bible tells of children being made to "pass through the fire"? How does textual evidence of this practice influence your understanding of the Bible?

---

13. Multiple texts attest to the practice of making children "pass through the fire" (e.g., Deut 18:10; 2 Kgs 16:2–3; 17:16–17; 21:6). However, these references usually appear in contentious passages suggesting that the writers did not approve of the practice. See Ackerman, *Under Every Green Tree*, 117.

2. In this story, the brother, Reuben, knowingly gives up his life for the sake of his clan. What sacrifices do we make for the good of others? What sacrifices do we expect others to make for us?

3. The narrator in this story, Reuel, truly believes that his brother's sacrifice will be efficacious and end the drought. What actions do we take and what results do we expect that are not entirely rational?

Bibliography

Ackerman, Susan. *Under Every Green Tree: Popular Religion in Sixth-Century Judah.* Harvard Semitic Monographs 46. Atlanta: Scholars Press, 1992.

Borowski, Oded. *Daily Life in Biblical Times.* Atlanta: Society of Biblical Literature, 2003.

Chilton, Bruce. *Abraham's Curse: Child Sacrifice in the Legacies of the West.* New York: Doubleday, 2008.

Day, John. *Molech: A God of Human Sacrifice in the Old Testament.* Cambridge: Cambridge University Press, 1989.

King, Philip J. and Lawrence E. Stager. *Life in Biblical Israel.* Louisville, Ky.: Westminster John Knox, 2002.

Marsman, Hennie J. *Women in Ugarit and Israel: Their Social and Religious Position in the Context of the Ancient Near East.* Oudtestamentische Studiën 49. Leiden: Brill, 2003.

Meyers, Carol L. *Discovering Eve: Ancient Israelite Women in Context.* New York: Oxford University Press, 1988.

Stager, Lawrence. "The Archaeology of the Family in Ancient Israel." *Bulletin of the American Schools of Oriental Research* 260 (1985): 1–35.

Sweeney, Marvin A. "Topheth." In *HarperCollins Bible Dictionary*, edited by Mark Allan Powell, 1059-60. 3rd ed. New York: HarperCollins, 2011.

He Didn't Name *Me*

I am Gomer

Emily Sher

1:2 The beginning of the LORD speaking to Hosea: The LORD said to Hosea: "Go, take for yourself a wife of whoredom and children of whoredom for the land is whoring from following after the LORD." 3 So he went and took Gomer,[1] daughter of Diblaim; and she conceived and bore him a son. 4 The LORD said to him, "Call his name 'Jezreel' for in a short time I will put the blood of Jezreel upon the house of Jehu, and I put an end to the kingdom of the house of Israel. 5 On that day I will break the bow of Israel in the valley of Jezreel."

6 She conceived again and gave birth to a daughter. He said to him, "Call her name 'Lo-ruhamah,' for I will no longer have compassion for the house of Israel nor will I forgive them."[2] 8 She weaned Lo-ruhamah, then she conceived and bore a son. 9 He said, "Call his name Lo-ammi because you are not my people and I will not be your God."

2:2 Be hostile against your mother, be hostile!

For she is not my wife

And I am not her husband

Then she will put away her whoring from her face

And her adultery from between her breasts.

---

1. "Gomer" comes from the Hebrew *gmr* meaning "to complete." The name of Hosea's wife can be understood to mean "enough," as a fitting response to the treatment that Gomer receives both in the biblical text and this story. See *HALOT* 1:197-98.

2. Scholars agree that Hosea 1:7 is a later addition to the text that diverts attention to Judah and war, hence its omission here.

3 Or else I will strip her naked

And expose her like the day she was born

And make her like a wilderness

And turn her into a land of drought

And kill her with thirst.

4 I will have no compassion on her children

For they are children of whoredom

5 Because their mother played the whore

She who conceived them has been put to shame

For she said, "I will go after my lovers

Who give me my food and my water

My wool and my linen

My oil and my drink."

6 Therefore, I will now hedge up her way with thorns

And I will wall up a wall against her

So she cannot find her pathways.

7 She will go after her lovers

but will not reach them;

She will seek them

but not find them.

Then she will leave and say,

"I will go and return to my first husband

for it was better for me then than now."

8 For she did not know

that it was I who gave her the grain, the new wine, and the fresh oil,

and lavished upon her gold and silver

that they used for the husband.

9 Therefore I will return and I will take back

my grain, in its time, and my new wine, in its season,

and I will snatch away my wool and my linen

that were to cover her nakedness.

10 Now I will uncover her shame

before the eyes of her lovers

and no husband will deliver her from my hand.

—HOSEA 1:2–6, 8–9; 2:2–10

I stood next to him, hands trembling and cold despite the desert heat—then I glanced at Hosea. Despite my thick veil he was somehow able to tell that I was nervous, and gave me a quick smile before returning to his usual expression: deep in contemplative thought, yet anxious. I drew my gaze back to the priest rather than look at the neighbors who had assembled to witness the marriage ceremony. I could feel Avram's stare on my back but refused to acknowledge him in return. Like generations of women before me, I was strong in my silence. This marriage was the only path that could save me and prevent shouts of "Whore!" from following me wherever I went. As the priest declared our union, the shouts were instead joyful . . . or was this the sound of audible relief? I was married and therefore saved.[3]

The simple ceremony passed in a blur until it was just me and my new husband, walking down the road. We travelled without a word until, clearly uncomfortable, Hosea broke the silence. "I know that you will not bleed tonight." With that simple sentence, he shocked me and my mouth dropped open. He knew?! Hosea's appearance in the village seemed out of nowhere. Yet he was aware of my reputation? Why then did he arrange with my father to wed me? I tried to think of something that I could use to defend myself and came up empty. Love would not work as an excuse, I knew that from experience. Clearly Hosea was still lost in thought, and started thinking out loud. "That is fine, that is fine . . . This marriage is fine, too. Yahweh has spoken to me about you . . . and why should I walk alone? It is a burden that so many prophets needlessly carry. Moses had Zipporah, Abraham had Sarah, and I found you praying so fervently, that must be a sign . . . ". My mind flashed back to that day weeks ago, when I had been pleading with Yahweh while tears streamed down my face.

‿

My brother and sister died when they were young. This left me an only child, and even more to my father's disappointment, a girl. He took out his anger at the diminished status of our family by refusing to acknowledge my mother or me, both of whom he blamed. My mother dealt with his dismissal by teaching me everything a woman should know, smoothing the rough places so I would be strong and survive. The first lesson was the power of silence. I have seen many women gain their power through

---

3. The Hebrew Bible does not offer any account of a wedding ceremony. Ivan Marcus points out that some narratives offer information on marriage customs, which focused on combining families. Usually marital arrangements were made by a paternal figure. For further discussion, see Marcus, *Jewish Life Cycle*, 124–33.

watchfulness and quiet acceptance. My mother said that by being an ideal wife, your husband, the clan, and eventually Yahweh would reward you. The second lesson was in technological skills; my mother taught me how to grind grain, make bread, spin wool, and weave cloth.[4] The third lesson was to respect my parents, and love and fear Yahweh.

I was five years old, and had just been instructed by my mother to stay silent in the face of trouble, when a glob of mud came flying through the air and landed on my best robe. A dark-haired, bright-eyed boy scampered from the olive grove. I gave him my best silent and judgmental stare before walking back toward my house. Suddenly—*thwack*—another glob smacked into my back. I took a deep breath, remembering my mother's lesson, when there was another thump on my legs. Furious, I whirled around. "Go eat locusts, you swine!" The boy stared back silently before bursting into laughter. He then grabbed my hand and ran, pulling me after him.

His name was Avram, and he was the eldest son of the wealthiest family in town. From that moment, we were inseparable. What he taught was completely different from my mother's lesson of silence. As years rolled on, Avram taught me how to track animals, find water in the desert, birth a ewe, and recognize edible plants. More importantly, he taught me to laugh, to smile, and to speak my own thoughts. With Avram, I could be myself. The feeling was exhilarating. And that is where my troubles began.

By the time of my first bleed, my father started entertaining marriage offers. This was my father's one chance to gain prestige through me. No offer was good enough for his daughter. Suit after suit was rejected and as every potential match dissolved, my hopes grew. Without admitting it to myself, I had been in love with Avram since that first glob of mud. Yet it was not my place to ask my father to talk to his father. So I just hoped.

Then one evening while I was silently cooking dinner with my mother, I noticed that my father had a guest with him in the courtyard. My attention was riveted as I watched my father and Avram's father share a cup of wine together, then embrace. Avram was there too, and he looked over at me, a large smile on his face. My father then called for me and my mother to come out and join the men. In those moments, my father looked at me with more tenderness than I had ever gotten from him. "You and Avram will marry within the month." My mother turned to me and murmured with a secret smile, "My daughter, this is the reward of silence."

4. Girls were trained from an early age in the skills they would need to help ensure a family's survival. For further discussion, see Ebeling, *Women's Lives in Biblical Times*, 43–60.

That night I met Avram in our usual spot, right outside of town. I ran straight into his arms and he spoke the words I longed to hear. "Gomer, I have loved you for years. I want to spend all my days with you." Promised seemed as good as married. When his lips met mine, I refused to turn away. The stars spun above us as I fell asleep in his arms.

I was awakened the next morning by a sharp tug on my arm. Startled, I shrieked as I was yanked upright. "You *whore*! How *dare* you? You have *ruined* our family!" My father was so furious that spittle was flying out of his mouth. He dragged me the rest of the way home and through his screaming and angry muttering I figured out the story. Late the night before, the midwife had been called to a house on the outskirts of town. She passed by Avram and me curled up together; by dawn the entire town had heard. Avram's father had then stormed into our home and called off the marriage. On his way out the door, he had turned to offer a chilling prediction: "Your daughter is useless. No upstanding man will have her now."

His prophecy proved true. Branded by the entire town, I soon discovered there would be no other marriage offers. My father's attitude towards me had always been icy but now my mother's anger was fresh and strong. Before she and I had always talked while working, and reserved our silence for the men. Now she also said nothing to me, and the isolation hurt more than blows. Even worse, I could no longer go to meet Avram. Those closest to me had abandoned me; what else could I do? I started to pray to Yahweh. I went to the place where Avram and I used to meet together, and let my prayers and tears flow. I asked for an escape—a way out of a family that despised me, a town that mocked me, and a friend who refused to acknowledge me. It was here that Hosea found me, on my knees, my eyes red and my face wet. I heard the sound of a man coming and looked up to see this stranger approaching me. He seemed the physical answer to my intangible prayers.

I knew who he was. The town had been talking about the prophet of Yahweh seen in this area, and this man fit the description: strong build, black curly hair, and a wild look in his eyes. Some were quick to insult him, disliking the message he preached. Others listened to him with growing unease yet newfound piety. The priests of Baal called him a false prophet while the priests of Yahweh extolled him as a chosen messenger.[5] But

---

5. The Canaanite storm god, Baal, was considered a threat to Yahwistic religion because many people believed in him. Baal is mentioned repeatedly as a target of Hosea's prophecy. For detailed discussion, see Herrmann, *DDD*, 132–39.

everyone agreed that he spoke with compelling conviction and had an aura of persistent intensity.

So when this man put out his hand to raise me from my knees, I took it. With so much gone, I thought, what did I have to lose? I would find out. But in that moment, I walked him back to my father's house and presented him to my parents. Hosea wasted no time. "Are you Diblaim?" he asked my father. My father, a bit overwhelmed at having this prophet appear in his house, just nodded. "I have come to take Gomer as my wife." How did he know my name? Relief washed over my father's face, and in a moment, the life I had known was over. I packed the few possessions I had—a change of clothes, a mat for sleeping, a jug for water—and carried them out of the house, following Hosea. I could see that my mother was crying, but she stayed silent. And now, so did I.

After the simple wedding ceremony, Hosea and I settled in his house, and fell into a routine. He traveled around the land preaching, while I stayed in our home. Our house was a few hours walk from the village where I grew up, but I refused to go back. This house was far from the others and I did not know what people in the nearest town knew of me. I could not bear to find out. So I stayed alone, constantly working to have enough food. Fortunately, there was a small stream near the house where I could get some water. I had learned from Avram how to scrounge plants in the area and tried to grow some myself. Sometimes I would find grain and oil near the house, maybe some cloth. Once there was even a small amount of silver and gold. I had no idea where it had come from, but I didn't care. I ate the food gratefully, and would ration it, never knowing if there would be more. Yet somehow, just when the grain was nearly gone, it would be replenished. I had experienced a miracle once before—when Hosea appeared out of no-where—and I had learned not to be surprised.

Still, mine was an isolated existence. In this solitude, I found out I was pregnant, about six full moons after our marriage. Hosea came home only once the entire time the new life was inside me, and said he would return for the birth of our first child. Just as his father had saved me, so too would this child, by giving me something to live for besides work and the rare visit from my husband. When the first of the birthing pains started, I was ready. I knew I might die, but that did not scare me. I lay down to endure the agony, be it new life or fresh death. My first child, a son, was born in a haze of pain and confusion. Sobbing and exhausted, after two days of labor, I finally held my son, then washed him carefully. He was strong and healthy—a perfect child with dark curly hair like his father and deep brown eyes that held wisdom.

Then, just as I raised my cleaned, precious infant to kiss his forehead, he was grabbed roughly from my arms. I looked up at the silhouette of a man and saw Hosea, holding our son awkwardly. Without tenderness, he explained, "Yahweh spoke to me. His name shall be Jezreel, for in a short time He will put the blood of Jezreel upon the house of Jehu, and put an end to the kingdom of the house of Israel." Stinging tears came to my eyes. Jezreel is where Jehu's bloody revolution started.[6] Why name a child after violence and bloodshed? Why must my beautiful son become the harbinger of the people's downfall?

As quickly as he came, Hosea was gone. I was left on my own with Jezreel for months. Every so often, Hosea would stay for a night, then disappear. Yet what could I say to him? He appeared to have little interest in me; often he acted as if in a trance. Years of practiced silence kept me from saying a word against him. I loved my son, but I was lonely and it was hard to survive, working by myself. I yearned for the day when Jezreel would be big enough to help me.[7]

In this time of lonely desperation, I bore another child. As with my first, I was alone for almost the entire pregnancy until the child was born. Then, as if from the sky, Hosea appeared and pulled my sweet baby girl from my arms. Her name was even worse than my son's. Hosea pronounced that our daughter would be called "Lo-ruhamah," for Yahweh would no longer have compassion for the house of Israel or forgive them. Lo-ruhamah means "not loved," and I battled my depression to prove her name wrong. My husband came back a few months later, as if he had been commanded to do so, and I was pregnant again.

One day, I was alone with Jezreel and Lo-ruhamah, my belly swelling with the third child, when I received a visitor. Occasionally people would pass by at a distance, but no one had ever before hiked up to our isolated house. I feared an intruder, but had to protect my children. I mustered my courage to face what came next, little suspecting who would stand before me. "Gomer?" the familiar voice asked.

"Avram?"

---

6. Jehu is the king of Israel in the 9th century BCE and Jezreel is where he staged the bloody coup that cemented his power (see 2 Kgs 9:10—10:11).

7. In ancient Israel, children were active workers and important contributors to the household economy. See Koepf-Taylor, *Give Me Children or I Shall Die*, 27–28.

He was still so handsome, and I knew in that moment that he had been supplying me with the secret provisions. Avram's first wife, whom he married shortly after I left the village, had died in childbirth with their son. He too had been terribly forlorn and, now a man, decided to come find me. Just as Hosea had saved me from my town, Avram rescued me from bitter isolation.

From that day on, Avram stopped by about once a week. He said nothing about the precious metal and did not seem to be returning for the money that I had found outside many moons ago. Rather, he played with my two children, helped me with my work, and made me laugh. I wanted to return the valuable metal to him, but knew he would not accept it from me. One day when Avram was outside the house, I had Jezreel put the silver and gold into his sack without saying a word. It was the best way I knew to thank him for his generosity. I loved having Avram near, yet I made him leave before the birth of my third child. I knew Hosea would return and not understand. If he saw any man, he would assume there were many.

As I expected, Hosea appeared when the child was born, to give an awful name to a sweet baby. He called our third child, "Lo-ammi," adding another grim declaration: "Israel is not Yahweh's people and Yahweh is not Israel's God." Even though his stay was brief, Hosea could tell there was something different about me. He looked at me with distrust. Perhaps he could see that I was stronger and didn't care as much about what he thought, as he angrily stalked out the door.

This time, Hosea stayed away for a very long period. There were no short nightly visits and I felt something was going to change for the worse. Even Avram could not pull me from my melancholy. Yet how could I be glad? My children's own names were reminders of how my people would be shunned by the God I loved, who had answered my prayers. Avram persisted in asking me what was wrong, and one day I shared my fears with him. "Oh Gomer," he whispered, "You have nothing to fear. Our God is slow to anger and abounding in loving kindness. Yes, our people have made mistakes. Aaron and the Israelites made a golden calf which caused Moses to cast down the rules given to him by God. Yet God forgave all of them.[8] He will forgive us for any wrongs we have done. What sin did these precious children commit to be named with such horrible prophecies?" His words were soothing, and he spoke of prosperity. Gently stroking my hair, he looked into my eyes, "One day you will eat the fruit of your own vine and sit under the shade of your own fig tree." I looked back at him with eyes full

8. See Exod 32:1–14.

of love. I was done with silence—it had only led to loneliness. I let myself love Avram.

I should have learned. The last time I was wrapped warmly and lovingly in Avram's arms, I became a social outcast. Hosea, with his impeccable timing, arrived at the same time as the midwife had so many years ago. When he saw Avram and me together, I was surprised that it was not hate or fury, but pain and hurt that covered Hosea's face. He looked as though he had just lost everything he believed in. For the first time, I saw that Hosea too could be silent. His head stayed erect, his eyes looking forward, but vacant. With a single tear sliding down his face, Hosea walked away. The children had been outside and I saw him stop to talk to them. They looked scared and confused—then their father was gone.

As soon as Hosea was out of earshot, Avram turned to me.

"We must get away. Grab the children. Like Hagar, we will find a way in the desert." I wanted to believe him, but I did not have that luxury. Three children depended on me.

"Avram, how do you not see? We are being punished by Yahweh. We have been together twice and both times Yahweh has sent suffering. We have broken the commandments. Go. Just go." And while my heart was breaking, he slowly turned and left.

I was again branded a whore, but this time it was far worse. Once he recovered from the shock, Hosea was filled with anger that rivaled the wrath of Yahweh. In his prophecies, Hosea talked about me and our children and our life together. He broadcast the words he had said to our children. Then I was no longer lonely, but surrounded by people who wanted to hurt me. For the first time in years, I returned—dragged to the village that I had escaped from long ago.

A great blur of color became individual images in bursts of clarity.

Burst: a large crowd jeering at me.

Burst: my mother sobbing.

Burst: Hosea, eyes bright with fury, gesturing wildly.

Burst: the crowd charging me, some men ripping my clothes and even tearing my skin.

Burst: a savage look on a young boy as he pelts me with a stone.

Burst: blood droplets on the sand next to my feet.

Burst: my children, sobbing, and thrust into the circle with me.

Burst: tears, unshed, in Hosea's eyes as he dragged me from the town.

Burst: I am in the dry and bristly wilderness. I am naked.

I do not even have a gourd for water.

I would have lain down and died if it were not for three pairs of eyes, all looking up at me as if I were their savior. Lo-ruhamah was holding Lo-ammi; they appeared weak and terrified. I knew that Jezreel wanted to be brave, but his eyes were filled with tears too. So I had no choice. I had to be the strong one, to keep my children alive. And so I pushed forward in the wilderness, with thorny bushes rising like walls. After walking with my children for hours, I found a small stream. I gathered some berries and fed them to my children, taking only enough for myself so I could nurse my baby son.

I had used two guiding principles in my life. First: silence will eventually be rewarded. Second: love shared with a man would bring me happiness. I had been foolish to have these beliefs. Both were proven false so I made a new principle: I would do everything for my children and they would survive. Their lives would come first. Somehow—another miracle—I managed to look at Jezreel, Lo-ruhamah, and Lo-ammi, and smile. I gathered my frightened and bewildered children there by the stream, hugged them, and told them everything would be alright. The children lay down, tired and confused but somehow heartened, and fell fast asleep. Once again, I started to pray, tears streaming down my face. However, this time they were tears of hope. Somehow I would find a way to create a life with my children. I fell asleep exhausted, but at peace. My new resolve had emboldened me.

Yet how dare I doubt Hosea's timing? When I heard a noise and opened my eyes, he was standing there, clutching our children to him. His tone was even.

"Count yourself blessed, Gomer. God told me to take you back." I stared at him in shock. He wanted me to return with him after beating me and publically stripping me naked while my children watched?! Was this a cruel joke?

I was glad that I had abandoned the habit of silence, because now the words tumbled out quickly. "Is this the same God that told you to beat me and cast me into the wilderness?"

Hosea looked uncomfortable. He muttered, "You broke Yahweh's laws. Punishment was deserved."

"Who decided this punishment?" I demanded.

"Well, Yahweh made the law . . . but I decided the punishment. I am Yahweh's prophet."

I was not done. "How dare you cast me away and shame me? Is that a marriage?! And now you say I should go back to you? Should the sheep return to the lion after it barely escapes with its life?" Chest heaving, I snatched back my children.

Hosea looked stunned. This was the most I had ever said to him. "Gomer, Yahweh commanded me to take you back." Then, if it is possible, he even looked ashamed. "Please, help me right this. I should not have hurt you as I did. Let me take you back in faithfulness."

I gave him a stone-cold stare.

He continued, "Do this for the children. You cannot survive out here for much longer. Let your children live."

I looked at my beloved, terrified children and sighed deeply. I had sworn to care for them. I had to hold on to the only conviction that had given me strength to live. I could return to Hosea or die.

And so, taking Lo-ammi in my arms, with Jezreel close to me on one side and Lo-ruhamah on the other, I followed Hosea. And as we walked, I talked, not prayed, to Yahweh. "For making this man your prophet, for giving him some of your power, I can never love or follow you again." My parents did not save me. My love did not save me. My husband cast me into the wilderness to die. And Yahweh told him what to do, then denied me safety. The only person I could rely on was myself.

So, with steady feet and a hardened heart, I followed my abuser home.

Discussion Questions

1. At points in this story, Gomer finds strength in remaining silent. Do you think that silence can be a source of power? When? How?

2. Both Yahweh and Hosea collude to abuse Gomer and punish her innocent children in this narrative. Do you think that the biblical text supports such a negative view of God and God's prophet? Why or why not?

3. Gomer suffers from Hosea's jealousy and ensuing domestic abuse. How might this story be used to help someone in an abusive relationship?

Bibliography

Ebeling, Jennie R. *Women's Lives in Biblical Times*. New York: T & T Clark, 2010.

Herrmann, Wolfgang. "Baal." Pages 132-38 in *DDD*.

Koepf-Taylor, Laurel W. *Give Me Children or I Shall Die: Children and Communal Survival in Biblical Literature*. Minneapolis: Fortress, 2013.

Marcus, Ivan G. *The Jewish Life Cycle: Rites of Passage from Biblical to Modern Times*. Seattle: University of Washington Press, 2004.

The Rich Young Man

Thoughts of the Mysterious Seeker

WILLIAM H. MOHR

17 As he [Jesus] was going out onto a road, a man came running up and kneeling before him asked him, "Good teacher, what must I do so that I may inherit eternal life?" 18 Jesus said to him, "Why do you call me good? No one is good, but God alone. 19 You know the commandments: 'You must not murder; You must not commit adultery; You must not steal; You must not testify falsely; You must not defraud; Honor your father and mother.'" 20 He said to him, "Teacher, I have kept all these from my childhood." 21 Jesus looked at him, loved him, and said to him, "You lack one thing—Go, sell whatever you have and give to the poor, and you will have treasure in heaven; and then follow me." 22 He was shocked by this message and went away grieving, for he had many possessions.

—*MARK 10:17–22*[1]

I, PALLADIUS, ARCHON OF Scythopolis, commence this scroll in this 17th year of the reign of Tiberius Caesar, as Herod Antipas is tetrarch of Galilee and Perea, Pontius Pilatus is procurator of Judea, in my 30th year of life, the 3rd anniversary of the death of my father Silvanus and my second

1. See also Matt 19:16–22 and Luke 18:18–23. In Luke's account the man who comes up to Jesus is described as a "ruler," as in this story.

89

year as archon, to reflect privately on matters of belief, the way of virtue and the meaning of the events that I am witnessing in Palestine.[2]

This is such a time—there are winds whipping about alternately carrying promise and peril, light and darkness. Dispatches have reached us from Herod which have been discussed in the council, about a prophet or holy man drawing many followers in Galilee with his teaching and amazing displays of power. The stories have made me quite curious. Who is this person that everyone is talking about? Are the rumors about his miracles true? Why does he speak of life after death? Are men to obtain life among the immortals? How could that be possible?! I must confess that my own education in philosophy and rhetoric gives me scant understanding to find answers. I do not hide the fact that I have a Jewish teacher and adviser here who has guided my study of certain texts of their scriptures. Their commandments are common knowledge in these parts, and seem largely to follow common sense. I have obeyed them throughout my life, albeit unknowingly. Their scrolls tell about one god that is as powerful as the entire Greco-Roman pantheon. This seems preposterous, yet I find more value in these readings and conversations than in any of our local rites and practices that have long honored Dionysus as the founder of this city.[3]

From the many reports that are circulating, I have gathered that this holy man is a common Galilean Jew, neither a scribe nor a Levite.[4] Thankfully, he is not inciting people against Rome as so many of these charismatic figures are wont to do. Yet his power, if it is not sorcery, can change death to life. There is a story, much talked about, that he revived the son of a widow

2. *Archon* is Greek for "leader" and served as a general title for a religious or governmental official. Scythopolis, also known as Beth-shean, was located to the east of the Jordan in a region of the Roman Empire comprised of ten cities and therefore called the Decapolis. After Herod the Great died in 4 BCE, his kingdom was divided among his four sons who ruled as tetrarchs. Herod Antipas governed the regions of Galilee and Perea until 34 CE. This story begins early in the year 30 CE, the 17th year of the reign of Tiberius as the Roman emperor, and the fourth year of Pontius Pilate as prefect (or governor) of Judaea.

3. Closely following rituals was considered more important than personal beliefs in Roman religion. Dionysus was the Greek god of ecstasy and is mentioned repeatedly in the books of Maccabees (2 Macc 6:7; 14:33; 3 Macc 2:29). For extended information about Dionysus and his cult, see F. Graf, "Dionysus," 252–58.

4. Scribes and Levites upheld Jewish ways of life. Levites were respected Jews descended from priestly lineage. In the Gospels, scribes are portrayed as teachers of Jewish tradition who have some political power and are often opposed to Jesus. Many likely served as low-level officials. Saldarini, "Scribes," para. 3.

at Nain, which is less than a day's journey north from here.[5] I heard this from a respected, local merchant and member of the council who trades in Nain and who related the excitement stirred there, although he did not himself meet this Jesus or witness any of his displays of power.

Both in accord with the dispatches that have reached me (and my own interest), I have instructed my men to gather information and alert me if this Jesus comes into town. If he determines to head south to Jerusalem for Passover, he must surely pass through here. When he does, I will have my own opportunity to assess his teaching and his powers to see if they are beyond those of a normal man. At this time, there are no instructions from the Sanhedrin or Pilatus to detain this Jesus.[6]

～

I have had discreet discussions with representatives of the Pharisee party of the Jews. They, like others, are in wonder at the teaching and works of this Jesus of Galilee. However, they disclaim him as being one of them. They say he consorts with unclean people and wrongly healed a man in the synagogue on the sacred day of rest, and there were many witnesses.[7] Their criticism seems entirely beside the point to me, just like the suggestion that a believer must be circumcised. Where could the power and message of Jesus come from, if not from the Jewish god? I do not credit the judgment of these Pharisees.

Jesus and his followers are reported in the Decapolis trans-Jordan.[8] They are not armed and he is gathering large crowds with his teaching. For this Jesus to be preaching in this area leads me to conclude that he is not limiting his teaching to the circumcised. If he is peaceable and can teach me what is most important from the Jewish teachings without submission to circumcision, I must go hear him. They say that Jesus is heading to Jerusalem so it will likely be only a matter of days before he is in the cardo preaching.[9] When he comes, I will ask his counsel. I will do this on my own account and will not approach him in the company of any of the scribes or Pharisees, lest he form the wrong impression.

5. See Luke 7:11–17. Nain is approximately twelve miles northwest of Scythopolis.

6. The Sanhedrin was a council of respected Jewish men that functioned as a court, hearing cases and delivering verdicts.

7. Mark 1:23–28; 3:1–5; 5:1–16.

8. Mark 10:1.

9. The cardo was the main street of a Roman city serving as the commercial artery, running north/south and often lined with merchants.

I am finished—I am humiliated—yet I am strangely not angry at Jesus. He taught in the cardo today and as I stood on the edge of the crowd, I was puzzled by the mundane questions that were put to him.[10] His gentle and firm authority was disarming and I felt strangely uncomfortable, so I left and went back to my office. A little later, my slave, whom I instructed to remain and monitor the events, ran in to tell me that Jesus had left the cardo and was heading to the *Via Jerusalem*. This was my chance. I had been thinking of what I wanted to ask him for weeks, and I knew I would regret it if I did not voice my question. I ran to find Jesus before he slipped away. Breathless, I finally caught up with him at the outskirts of town.

I think it was only his disciples who heard our exchange. What a shabby and dusty bunch of Galileans. They would be well matched to caravan camels! They just stood there gaping at me, even though I knelt before Jesus to show respect.[11] I hope that I was not seen doing that, although some of my citizens will probably learn of the meeting and laugh behind my back. Making jokes at my expense! Surely some will report my unbecoming behavior of running through the streets.

I addressed him: "Good teacher, what must I do so that I may inherit eternal life?"

His response immediately disoriented me: "Why do you call me good? No one is good, but God alone."

Was he implying that no one can be good? What value is his teaching if no one can be good? But he went on and I continued to listen. He then reviewed the Jewish commandments and my heart rose, as I have honored these faithfully. I have my position in this town because no one can reproach my conduct. On my father's grave, this is true!

So I replied, "Teacher, I have kept all these from my childhood."

He looked at me with a tenderness that shocked me. I didn't trust myself to speak. Next the blow: "You lack one thing—Go, sell whatever you have and give to the poor and you will have treasure in heaven; and then follow me."

His countenance made my heart want to follow him. He did not demand that I do any of these things, but his eyes penetrated me and I knew in that instant that he was giving the verdict of heaven.

Then reality set in. How could I possibly do this? After a moment, my chin sank and my expression must have betrayed me; Jesus stepped past me

10. Mark 10:2–16.

11. Mark 10:17.

without saying another word. He departed our city. His teaching is more demanding than anything I have ever heard from any rabbi or scribe. Yes, I know of the Jews in the desert who have broken with the world and live a hard-scrabble life.[12] Does he mean that I should join them?

But his suggestion is impossible for me. My office is due to my rank and the income from my properties and businesses. Without my properties my wife would go back to her family. What would become of our children? My constructions in the cardo, the forum, and the baths would all cease. Should I be reduced to the level of these dirty, illiterate Galileans? Is that existence the rightful destiny of man? I think not. Perhaps my Aramaic is failing me and I have misunderstood the prophet. But he is gone and I have been left with my resources and nagging thoughts. I am troubled that he may speak the truth.

↩

The news has reached me that Jesus was crucified in Jerusalem on the eve of Passover a fortnight ago. It is all madness! He did not lead an insurrection. It seems like another episode in an unending chain of unseemly Jewish squabbles. Herod's attachés sent a note trying to make light of the situation, saying that the indictment on the cross sardonically proclaimed: "King of the Jews."[13] Still, they are advising watchfulness; there may be an uprising in Galilee since this "king" has been crucified. Pilatus added a cryptic note speculating that this may not be the end of the Jesus matter.

I am surprised that this news disturbs me so. I keep remembering his countenance that day when we spoke so briefly. I have decided to head up to Jerusalem for Pentecost. As long as things remain quiet here, I can leave my adjutant in charge here with the Roman cohort at his disposal. I need to get more knowledge of what is actually happening.

↩

Here in Jerusalem, I discovered that the Jesus followers were gathering in a room of a large house. My slave, who had accompanied me to Jerusalem, led me to this building. When I finally arrived it was very crowded, but people could see that I was a man of position and made space for me to enter. A few moments later, there was a sudden rushing wind, which seemed

---

12. The community at Qumran was a quasi-monastic Jewish sect that lived in the desert. Many scholars believe they are responsible for the Dead Sea Scrolls. For discussion of this community's rejection of wealth, see Magness, *Stone and Dung,* 12–13.

13. Mark 15:26.

very odd since it was a calm day outside. Then I saw something like flames on certain heads, although surely this was just my eyes playing tricks on me. How could this possibly be? Yet I questioned my own thinking because everyone started exclaiming about what was happening. Even more curious, we all understood each other, regardless of our native tongue: Asians, Parthians, Egyptians, Libyans and many others! Some people sneered that it was just a drunken melée, but I swear that I could understand foreigners.[14]

Then a man who wore no priestly garb or sign of any rank stood up to speak. He was bearded, thickly-built with exposed, muscled arms, with which he gesticulated. I suspected immediately that this man was a Galilean fisherman of the Jesus party, as his words soon confirmed. He had such authority that a silence fell over the room that had been filled with pandemonium just a few moments before. People hung on his words—as did I. Occasionally questions were shouted and he patiently wove those into his presentation about Jesus. His voice rose and fell as he explained that Jesus was the chosen instrument of God's mercy and love, and that Jesus had been raised from the dead and was rejoined with God in heaven. He shared the words of the prophets and the promises to David, which he claimed that Jesus fulfilled.[15] It was hard not to be captivated by his message because of his passion and conviction.

The Jesus followers asked nothing of the crowd save to be reconciled to God and to be baptized. The pool in the courtyard of the house became thronged with those who were being baptized, and an undeniable energy pervaded the place. I drew near to observe the baptizing, recalling Jesus' words to me that I renounce my possessions. Then I stepped forward and they gave the baptism without any oath or payment required. I was surprised to see my slave step forward and be baptized as well.

⟿

While still in Jerusalem, I arranged a private meeting with the head of the Jesus party, the fisherman I previously noted, who is Simon Peter.[16] My

14. Acts 2:1–13.

15. Acts 2:14–36.

16. Simon Peter (also called Cephas) is the most prominent of Jesus' disciples, apparently the leader. The earliest New Testament writings, the undisputed letters of Paul, refer to him repeatedly (see 1 Cor 15:3–5; Gal 1:18; 2:7–12); the Gospels and the book of Acts contain many more references. Some readers are confused because this disciple has three names that can appear interchangeably. "Simon" is his Jewish name; Simeon was a son of Jacob and Leah (see Gen 29:33). "Cephas" is his Aramaic name (Jesus and his disciples spoke Aramaic). "Peter" is his nickname (analogous to "Rocky"); *petra* is Greek for "rock."

slave had made inquiries to discern where they were lodging. I also met Peter's brother, Andrew.[17] I gained great peace from my discussion with them. They do not bear arms nor do they seek any revenge on the Jews or Romans who collaborated in the death of Jesus. Peter's instruction gave me consolation in explaining that for man it is impossible to perfect oneself, but everything is possible through the merciful care of God.

I have come to believe that Jesus was a son of God clothed in power and wisdom. I felt reconciled from years of spiritual wandering when Peter baptized me and my slave in the company of the other disciples. He did not require me to swear an oath to give away my properties, though I promised to provide him with some level of support. He is familiar with my city and my office there; I can be useful to him and offer him protection in his journeys to and from his home at Bethsaida.[18]

I will help Simon Peter because I believe his sincerity. In truth, I still wonder if Jesus is indeed the Messiah who fulfills the Jewish scriptures. Many people have become convinced by Jesus' miracles and those that his followers still manage to perform. Yet for me, a baptized believer, it was that day—even that moment—when Jesus looked into my eyes that ultimately led me to associate with this motley band.

Discussion Questions

1. In Mark 10:21 the Greek clearly specifies that Jesus looked at the man and "loved him" (a form of the word *agape*). Does it strike you as strange that Jesus would love this man at first glance? Why do you think the text includes this powerful detail?

2. Even though the man in this story is eager to inherit eternal life, he does not take Jesus' advice. Can you blame him for not selling everything? What would you do if Jesus gave you the same instructions?

3. As the story continues, this powerful man decides to become a follower of Jesus when doing so requires only professing faith and being baptized,

17. The Gospels of Matthew and Mark report that Simon Peter and his brother Andrew were fishers who followed Jesus together (see Matt 4:18–20; Mark 1:16–18). Luke and John also note that they are brothers (Luke 6:14; John 1:40–44).

18. See John 1:44. Bethsaida was a village located on the shore of the Sea of Galilee, which Jesus may have visited repeatedly (Mark 6:45; Luke 9:10). Strange, "Bethsaida" n.p., *ABD on CD-ROM*.

not selling his possessions or becoming circumcised. Does faith become worth less when it requires less? Why or why not?

Bibliography

Graf, F. "Dionysus." Pages 252-58 in *DDD*.

Magness, Jodi. *Stone and Dung, Oil and Spit: Jewish Daily Life in the Time of Jesus*. Grand Rapids, Mich.: William B. Eerdmans, 2011.

Saldarini, Anthony J. "Scribes." In *ABD on CD-Rom*.

Strange, James F. "Bethsaida." In *ABD on CD-Rom*.

Revelation

EVAN CAMERON

16 Then the soldiers led him into the courtyard (that is, the Praetorium), and they called together the whole cohort. 17 They dressed him in purple; and after plaiting a crown of thorns, they put it on him. 18 And they began to salute him, "Hail, King of the Jews!" 19 They struck his head with a reed, and spat on him, and knelt on their knees and worshipped him. 20 And when they had mocked him, they stripped him of the purple cloak and put his own clothes on him. And they led him out to crucify him.

21 They compelled a passer-by, Simon of Cyrene—who was coming from the country, father of Alexander and Rufus—to carry his cross. 22 Then they brought Jesus to the place Golgotha, which is translated: Place of a Skull. 23 They gave him wine mixed with myrrh, but he did not take it. 24 And they crucified him, and divided his clothes, casting lots among them for what each should take. 25 It was the third hour when they crucified him. 26 The inscription of the accusation against him read, "The King of the Jews." 27 With him they crucified two thieves, one on his right and one on his left.[1]

29 Those who passed by reviled him, shaking their heads and saying, "Ah! The one who would destroy the temple and build it in three days!" 30 "Save yourself!" "Come down from the cross!" 31 Likewise the high priests, with the scribes, were mocking him among themselves

---

1. Some ancient manuscripts add v. 28: "And the Scripture was fulfilled which says, 'And he was reckoned with transgressors.'"

saying, "He saved others; he cannot save himself. *32* Let the Messiah, the King of Israel, come down now from the cross so that we may see and believe." Those who were crucified with him taunted him.

33 When it was the sixth hour, darkness came over the whole land until the ninth hour. *34* At the ninth hour Jesus cried out with a loud voice, "Eloi, Eloi, lema sabachthani?" that is translated: "My God, my God, why have you abandoned me?" *35* When some of the bystanders heard it, they said, "Look, he is calling for Elijah!" *36* Someone ran, filled a sponge with sour wine, put it on a stick, and gave it to him to drink, saying, "Wait! Let us see if Elijah will come to take him down." *37* Then Jesus let out a loud cry and breathed his last. *38* And the curtain of the temple was split in two, from top to bottom.

39 Now when the centurion, who stood over against him, saw that he breathed his last in this way, he said, "Truly this person was the son of God!"

—MARK 15:16-39

MY HONOR WAS AS invisible as my breath—yet just as vital. As a soldier of Rome, I gladly paid the price of blood on my hands for the honor of my name.[2] Although I owed my father respect as my elder, we both knew that the people of our village held me in higher esteem than him. This had always been my dream, and it was my father's dream too. He was a poor fisherman; I was among the empire's elite. Even more impressive, I was a centurion, an esteemed military officer, stationed in the conquered city of Jerusalem.[3]

I had earned my title through war. I never cared about whom we were fighting, only desiring the wild energy of combat. The memory of my first

2. In ancient Mediterranean honor/shame culture, "prestige derives from the domination of persons rather than things." Malina, *New Testament World*, 37.

3. Those who volunteered for the Roman army would enlist for a long period, initially sixteen years, although this commitment frequently lengthened to twenty or twenty-five. Benefits for Roman soldiers included regular pay, occasional bonuses, good lodging with bath houses, medical care, clothing and equipment provisions, a discharge bounty for life after the army, and legal provisions and tax exemptions for veterans. Centurions were among the top-ranking soldiers, earning many multiples the pay of regular enlisted men. This afforded them noted status in the military and civilian life, along with considerable wealth. See Kennedy, "Roman Army," 790-91.

battle, at Idistavisus,[4] is still fresh. Rain poured from the summer sky as earth and men mixed in a frenetic haze of greys and browns. We trammeled the invading enemy on the northern edge of the Empire's borders. Lusting for blood, I charged against the nameless foes. Hesitation was death; I chose power, action, survival.

"Stab whatever moves close to you! Honor is yours today, men of Rome!" our officer yelled as we entered that first fight. With animal ferocity, I attacked without mercy. Flashes of silver sword added bright crimson to muddy pools. Fighting turned to strangling brawls in the sloppy field. As if in slow motion, we lunged against strangers. Faces were choked in mud, until they went lifeless. How many did I kill? There was no time to count in that wasteland of battered corpses where everything was brutal aggression. The wet ground sucked at our shoes and our human capacity for mercy. We knew that the loss of a mere individual—even our own lives—was nothing in the context of empires.

ᦔ

Rome was an empire of precise justice and order, and I loved my work serving this system. The efficient existence of a soldier suited me well. We ate decent food; we received sufficient clothing rations; we killed for our emperor. I was one of the physically strongest of our century,[5] allowing me to win any one-on-one fight on the battlefield. The honor and wealth grew each year, carrying me far beyond the destiny of my meager father and his poor, salty boats. For years I gladly traded blood for honor, climbing ranks from average to extraordinary. All this killing was rewarded the day I was finally granted the title of centurion. However, I was disappointed to be assigned to a little-known part of the Empire.

"Jerusalem will suit you, Marcellus," I was told by my own centurion before being sent to this new land. He informed me that it was the home of Jews who worshipped their god and were exempt from military service,

---

4. In 16 CE fifty thousand German tribesmen and seventy-four thousand Roman fighters met at the Battle of Idistavisus along the Weser River (in contemporary Germany). Germanicus Caesar, the adopted son of Emperor Tiberius, led the Romans against Arminius, head of the Germanic men. "The struggle between 128,000 men went on for hours." Dando-Collins, *Legions of Rome*, 269. The Germanic tribes experienced massive casualties and lost the battle.

5. A century was a unit of 100 soldiers in a Roman legion, hence the commander was a centurion. Powell, "Centurion," 125.

unlike other conquered peoples.[6] "We are all invasive foreigners to them. Expect hostility. Show them Roman strength as you have in battle here."

And so I fulfilled my commission, traveling to this arid outpost and bringing the military power and honor of all Rome with me. Marked by my uniform and thereby instantly recognized as elite, I ventured into this world of peasants who worshipped some strange god whose name I did not recognize.

One of my duties as the centurion of Jerusalem was to conduct executions for my superior, Pontius Pilate. This governor of the Judea province was renowned for his violent handling of Jewish resistance to Roman rule.[7] I enjoyed serving him because executions offered a break from the otherwise boring days patrolling these hot streets filled with poor, uninteresting people.

I would round up the criminals who were slaves or foreigners and Pilate would pronounce the sentence. Crucifixions were popular and effective; public torture and agonizing death efficiently quelled resistance to Roman rule. Hills made the executions easy to see. In my aching for battle, I looked forward to the end of the week when these killings took place and my warrior aggression resurged within me. Many of those executed pleaded that they were innocent of any crime, but why should I care about these non-citizens? I paid no mind to their pitiful cries; crucifixions were as mindless as battlefield killings. All for the glory of Rome.

I came to Pilate's palace one Friday to prepare for the three crucifixions planned for that day. I immediately realized that for some reason these executions would be different; large crowds had gathered around the building. Those gathered moved restlessly with wild eyes. I had seen this look before, in soldiers before battle, when men became animals hunting for survival.

I didn't care what they were yelling about. No Roman officer would listen to the cries of a foreigner. I strode inside the palace as usual, although this time I was quickly approached by an exasperated Pilate.

"Marcellus, go, get Barabbas, release him to me," he commanded, turning and hastily walking away.

"Barabbas? He is to be crucified today." I remained calm, masking my disappointment. I hoped Pilate had made a mistake. I did not want to be deprived of some of the day's violent action.

6. "Jews were long exempted from military service to Rome . . . they had no family links or shared values with the troops in the province." Kennedy, "Roman Army," 794.

7. Philo, a Hellenistic Jewish philosopher of the first century, writes that Pilate was known for "his violence, his abusive behavior, his frequent executions of untried prisoners, and his endless savage ferocity." Schwartz, "Pontius Pilate," 398.

He spun and shot back: "Do not question me! All day people have dared to act as if they can influence me! Now you too? You question my authority!?" Pilate was irate.

"No sir." A military man always knows his place.

"Yes, Barabbas! And now a new man will be crucified instead! The soldiers will bring him to you after the flogging."

I knew that Barabbas was one of the most violent men we had ever detained, determined to lead Jewish revolt against Rome at all costs. Some said that he was the son of a renowned rabbi,[8] but from my perspective blood was blood. I didn't care who we killed and my mood revived in knowing that his crucifixion had been replaced by that of another criminal. I would have an interesting day after all.

I walked down the damp corridor of waste-covered cells. Calling off the guards outside his cell, I opened the door to find the prisoner to be released. Barabbas's eyes flickered as his tongue dashed quickly across his teeth. Blood still stained his skin from his fight with my men, where he had wildly stabbed at them before being captured. The room was swollen with smells of rotted flesh and echoes of forsaken souls.

"Get up," I commanded him. "You are free to go."

I had thought he would be grateful and humbly walk out of this hell-hole, but instead his sinister laughter reverberated off the walls of the small cell, intensifying the nauseating smell.

I retained my composure. "It is the will of Roman empire that you be released."

Now Barabbas responded. "Freedom?" He laughed again. "It doesn't exist. Not here. You taught us that, soldier, with your sword and your crosses."

I found myself strangely engaged by this surprisingly coherent criminal and could not help myself from defending Rome. "We give you roads, protection, structure! You live as a criminal. That is no fault of mine."

"We both seek to kill. Your killing gives you honor, but mine brings crucifixion. You think you are that different from me?" Again he mocked me with laughter.

Why should I tolerate such talk? I took a step into the cell and slammed my fist into his gut, knocking him to his knees. "You will show me the honor I deserve! Get up and get out." His weakened body rose too

---

8. The word *bar* means "son" and *Abba* means "father," a title used for esteemed teachers. The text gives no information about Barabbas besides his name. See Wilkins, "Barabbas," n.p., *ABD on CD-ROM*.

slowly, so I grabbed him by his bony collarbone and threw him out of the cell. Barabbas tried to speak but had no breath left. I was glad to silence another local rebel and left him for the guards to remove from the jail, then made my way to Pilate.

I found the governor in his headquarters, where he instructed me to move on to Barabbas's replacement. Pilate assured me that this peasant had been flogged well and instructed me, "Find this convicted man and take him up the high hill of Golgotha. Crucify him there so the crowds can see."

My hands were still shaking in anger. These miserable commoners showed no gratitude for the peaceful existence within our borders that the Roman Empire offered them. I was happy to kill today. Jerusalem needed to see the authority of a centurion.

I followed my command and found the newly accused criminal barely standing in the courtyard, wearing a loose tunic that had been tossed over him to parade him through the street.

My soldiers had gathered for the day's work and a few of them smiled at my arrival. A well-respected soldier called to me, "Marcellus, look at this Jew! Claims he is a king, but his followers deserted him." Grinning, I walked in and joined them.

"Well!" I said to my soldiers, "Let's show this king the honor he deserves! Dress him like royalty!"

We tore off the prisoner's tunic, knocking his weakened body to the ground. His lacerated and bleeding back and legs showed that Pilate was right; the flogging had been very thorough.[9] My men spat upon his nakedness, taking out their aggressive energy on this worthless foreigner. I forced the man to his feet and commanded one of my soldiers to fetch the purple robe that was lying in a heap in the corner of the courtyard. Pilate had been wearing it and tossed it on the ground. He would not miss it; he had so many royal cloaks, and we were amusing ourselves with this "king." Since he was too battered to move much, a few of us worked together to put the purple robe on this bloody prisoner. My soldiers were enjoying this diversion and I was glad to reward them for their hard work by letting them have their fun. One of my soldiers ran to the scribal room of the palace and had someone there quickly write out on a piece of papyrus, "King of the Jews." The soldier grabbed the sign and a long reed, which he took back to the

9. A person to be flogged was stripped then had his hands tied to an upright post. The back, buttocks, and legs would be whipped with "braided leather of variable length, in which small iron balls or sharp pieces of sheep bones were tied at intervals." Edwards et al., "Physical Death," 1457.

courtyard and placed in the criminal's hand. Here was the king's title and scepter—we roared with laughter! Another soldier ran to the garden and cut off some thorny branches with his sword, then wove them into a spikey crown that he thrust roughly on the criminal's head. His scalp immediately begin to bleed as he slowly stood, hunched over, before us.

"Look at the king!" I jeered at him. "Come to his throne with your requests!"

A few soldiers came forward. "Prophesy to us!" one bellowed as we laughed. The soldier leaned close and slapped the criminal, sharp, across the cheek. "Who hit you, king of the Jews?" Another slap, fiercer this time. "Who hit you! Prophesy!"

Their ferocious energy fed on itself as the spitting continued, chunks of mucous hitting the mouth and eyes of the "king" as the soldiers screamed in his face. A young soldier took the reed from the condemned man's hand and struck his head. He collapsed to the courtyard floor out of weakness. I mockingly fell to my knees before this bleeding and bruised figure lying on the ground. "Hail the King of the Jews!" We laughed all the more; he quietly wept. Blood soaked through the purple robe on the man's back as he breathed heavily, seeking to get to his feet, crawling, knees and hands holding him up.

After a while of this playing, attention to the game began to wane and we needed to get our job done.

I reclaimed my authority. "We can't kill him yet; he needs to carry his cross up the hill. Put his clothes back on him. Go get the two others to be crucified. I'll meet you on the road toward Golgotha."

The soldiers did as I instructed then left the courtyard; one took the sign with him, and suddenly it was very quiet. All I heard were the quiet sobs coming from the man on the floor.

Into the silence, he spoke for the first time, his voice barely a whisper: "I forgive you."

Shocked, I whirled my head around to look at this bleeding figure on the floor. "Be silent and prepare for your death! Your words are nothing to me."

"Sooner than you think, you will know who is speaking to you. . . ." His voice was labored. "And then," he added, "Then you will beg . . . to listen to me again." His voice trailed off.

Beg? From a criminal!? This insult was outrageous, but my curiosity was piqued by his desire to talk to me. Mustering more strength, the bloodied man continued in gasps.

"My friend, you will do more than beg. You will be . . . my disciple."

How dare he call me a friend! I would become *his* disciple? My curiosity was replaced by rage.

But then I caught myself. Why did I care? He was nobody. I was the centurion in charge and there was no need to get riled by some prisoner.

I issued my orders. "Get up. We're leaving."

I started out of the courtyard, this man stumbling after me. Even though walking took so much of his remaining strength, he continued to try to talk to me.

"To heal . . . to forgive . . . this is the path to honor."

I turned back on him with fresh anger. "Who are you to speak about honor *to me*? You know nothing of honor! Prepare to die a painful, shameful death."[10]

He met my fierce gaze with calm eyes and stayed silent. I turned and walked out of the courtyard, commanding soldiers just outside the palace to get this man and force him to join the march to the hill.

I led us on the path to Golgotha, bringing a crowd: the three accused men, my soldiers, and locals who had gathered outsider the governor's palace earlier and followed to witness the killings. The prisoner who had been flogged so much was too weak to carry his own cross, so I picked a face out of the crowd and threatened him to carry a cross or feel my sword.[11] He silently picked up the heavy wood and walked with us.

It was still morning. We arrived at Golgotha, and offered all three criminals a bitter mix of wine and gall.[12] The man exchanged for Barabbas refused to drink; he did not seem to care about reducing the pain. My soldiers then pushed the three criminals to the ground with their backs against their crosses. The two other criminals, knowing that these were their last moments of freedom, began to fight back. This kicking and biting was normal, as they exercised the final use of their limbs. Their struggles

10. "As crucifixion damaged no vital organs, death could come slowly, sometimes after several days of atrocious pain." O'Collins, "Crucifixion," 1209. To purposely drag out the pain, a small board was attached to the cross as a rough seat, drawing out the asphyxiation process. Edwards et al., "Physical Death," 1459.

11. See Mark 15:21.

12. This drink could have mild numbing effects to decrease awareness of pain. Edwards et al., "Physical Death," 1459.

would end momentarily. As centurion, I had seen this many times since I ensured that the condemned are properly nailed to the crossbar. I ordered three soldiers to hold each man down. I started with the two criminals who were showing resistance. I found the nailing spot, below the wrist and between the two bones, and pounded the metal spikes, about the length of a human hand, through the men's wrists.[13] With each spike strike, the men screamed at me, cursing Rome, cursing death.[14] My hands red with blood, I turned to the battered man from the courtyard.

Slowly, I walked over to him, lying on the ground, tied to his cross. He had just witnessed the horror of the two men before him, yet he seemed strangely calm. I called the soldiers off, kneeling beside him with the spikes. They went over to the heap of the prisoners' clothes and starting arguing about who got what. Eventually they decided to cast lots.

With my soldiers' attention elsewhere, I paused to look at this prisoner with an air of purpose, even in these brutal moments. This was the closest I had physically been to him all day. I took his arm, and he looked at me, tears welling up from his eyes. I could see the fear, and remembered his words earlier: "*I forgive you.*"

My focus fractured. His raw display of humanness awakened a new and uncomfortable feeling within me. I fumbled with the spike, losing my firm grip. My hands trembled. I swung at the nail with hesitation, missing it. The hammer fell with a dull thud into the dirt. I picked it up and swung again with uncommon weakness; again I missed.

Having divided the clothes, the soldiers glanced back at me.

"Come on Marcellus, do it!" one impatient soldier called.

I shook my head, breaking eye contact with the man lying on the cross. Holding his wrist in place, I did my duty. The heavy hammer met the spike. Blood burst out of his arm, streaming down to the wood and earth below. His arm flexed as I pierced it, and he screamed loudly in sudden agony.

With one arm nailed, I took the other, stretching it wide across the wood. His body was shaking in pain, yet again he did not resist me. I felt his trembling, and I again lost control. I had never hesitated at a crucifixion before—why was this time different? I looked up and noticed an unnatural

---

13. Only nailing through the wrist, not the palms, could support the weight of the hanging body. Edwards et al., 1460.

14. This act would "sever the rather large median nerve. The stimulated nerve would produce excruciating bolts of fiery pain in both arms." Ibid.

darkness in the sky for this early in the afternoon. My usual adrenaline had been replaced with an unusual anxiety. What was I doing to this man?

My damp palms again faltered with the spike. It slipped from my hands, bouncing off the wood to the ground. My reflexes were slow to pick it up; the air felt heavy and hard to navigate.

"DO IT!" came the cries all around me. Did I imagine it, or were these chants real? I felt drunk, paralyzed by inner confusion meeting outside expectation. Sweating, I found the spike in the dirt.

"Honor . . . must maintain honor," I whispered to myself. Discipline. Honor. Rome. Grabbing his other arm, I drove the spike into his flesh. The soldiers cheered. The one who had carried the "King of the Jews" sign quickly nailed it to the top of this cross. I wanted this ordeal to be over. My job was nearly done.

"Raise them up!" I commanded quickly to my soldiers. I needed to show control of the situation; surely others had seen my hesitation. Once the crosses were vertical, I drove similar spikes through the feet to make them flat against the wood, left foot above the right.

Darkness was continuing to trickle across the sky, as if the clouds too had been poisoned with this man's lost blood. The frenzy of death was building in the screams of pain from the men crucified beside this "King of the Jews." The crowd who had followed us up the hill now had their chance to join in the event. These bystanders shook their heads, mocking his lacerated body and laborious breaths.

"Ah! The one who would destroy the temple and build it in three days!"
"Save yourself!"
"Come down from the cross!"

Now nature came to inflict pain. Insects swarmed around his bleeding head, wrists, back and feet. He wailed in agony with every breath, putting painful weight on his only source of leverage: the nailed feet and wrists. The open wounds on his back scraped against the rough wood.[15] Every few seconds this upward motion was necessary or suffocation would be instant.

15. In order to exhale, the crucified person needed to lift the body by pushing with the feet and wrists. This triggered four sources of searing pain: the nailed sites of both wrists and the feet, as well as scraping the open wounds on the back. Eventual suffocation, joined with blood loss, would be the actual cause of death: "Each respiratory effort would become agonizing and tiring and lead eventually to asphyxia." Edwards et al., "Physical Death," 1461.

Some of the religious officials were there. A few of them had found this man threatening and wanted to make sure of his doom. They joined in the derision.

"He saved others—he can't save himself!" they called, their voices dripping with condescension.

"Let the Messiah, the King of Israel, come down now from the cross so that we may see and believe." Their tone was vindictive.

Even the other men being crucified managed to speak enough to join in insulting him.

"Save yourself . . . save us—what kind of king are you?"

"No king at all!"

I felt myself beginning to separate from this taunting crowd. They felt hatred. . . . What was I feeling? Could it be sympathy?

A few hours passed as blood and sweat kept falling from this man, small drops splashing into the earth. The agony was worsening. Shudders of pain rippled across his crucified body, diffused only by the tight nails binding his limbs. His face was marked with tears and blood, cutting trails of clean streaks against the dirt on his cheeks and temples.

The infection of darkness continued its spread across the afternoon sky. For the first time, an awful feeling of doubt filled my mouth with the taste of bile. Was this justice? Was this honor? I tried to find my voice to join my soldiers or the crowds. Yet in these moments, unsettling questions were arising within me. How could this killing be honorable? What kind of man would forgive his merciless executioner?

Unexpectedly, the man occupying my thoughts suddenly called out to the sky from his position above us: "My God, my God, why have you abandoned me?" His loud voice got the attention of the crowd, who used his words as fodder for further scorn.

"Look, he is calling for Elijah," one of the religious leaders noted sardonically. Someone ran to him, lifting up a sponge with sour wine on the end of a long stick as a drink. Was this a mocking of some ritual?

"Wait! Let us see if Elijah will come to take him down," a priest called in mean playfulness, while the stick was being poked toward the man's mouth.

And then, with a loud cry, the man breathed his last breath.[16] I had seen this many times, when the final shudder goes through the body and the rattle of death comes out through the mouth. A deep sigh—then stillness.

16. The time it took to die from crucifixion was "inversely related to the severity of the scourging." Edwards et al., "Physical Death," 1460. Jesus' relatively quick death suggests a

Yet something was happening beyond what was going on here.

I was unable to move. Why did this man make me doubt all I had known? My heart felt constricted, as if it were balled up into a tight fist. I couldn't breathe. The truth of realization was before my eyes in the shape of a dead man; my powerful honor was made foolish by the mercy of a powerless peasant.

I had killed so many men, but nothing had prepared me for a man who forgave me. Who was this person? Why did he affect me so? Was he more than a mortal? In a moment of piercing recognition, I realized what I had done.

Weakened by my own agony, I fell on my knees for the second time that day in front of this man. I looked up at the dead prisoner hanging in front of me and yelled to the darkened sky, "Truly, this man was the son of God!"

The soldiers looked at me, bewildered. I had never flinched from loyalty to Rome, never once shown weakness. How could a centurion, the most honorable and professional of all Roman soldiers, possibly be so vulnerable?

But I just crumbled, a human heap beneath that cross, and sobbed.

Who am I to be forgiven?

Discussion Questions

1. Did you realize that crucifixions were so common or so gruesome? Does this knowledge influence your understanding of Jesus' death at all? If so, how? If not, why not?

2. The centurion holds power as a foreigner dominating an indigenous culture. Where do you see this pattern today? Can leaders like Jesus be effective in such a culture? Why or why not?

3. While execution by crucifixion is ancient, execution by the state still exists in over half of the United States. Do you think that society has made significant progress over the last two thousand years in its treatment of criminals? Why or why not?

---

brutal flogging earlier in the day.

Bibliography

Dando-Collins, Stephen. *Legions of Rome*. London: Quercus, 2010.

Edwards, William, Wesley Gabel, and Floyd Hosmer. "On the Physical Death of Jesus Christ." *JAMA* 255 (1986) 1455–63.

Kennedy, David. "Roman Army." In *ABD* 5:789–98.

Malina, Bruce. *The New Testament World*. Louisville: Westminster John Knox, 2001.

O'Collins, Gerald. "Crucifixion." In *ABD* 1:1207–10.

Powell, Mark Allan, ed. *HarperCollins Bible Dictionary*. 3rd ed. New York: HarperCollins, 2011.

Schwartz, Daniel. "Pontius Pilate." In *ABD* 5:395–400.

Wilkins, Michael J. "Barabbas." In *ABD on CD-ROM*.

How Did He Know?

LAWRENCE BARTLEY

25 Just then a lawyer stood up testing him [Jesus], saying, "Teacher, what shall I do to gain eternal life?" 26 He said to him, "What is written in the law? What do you read?" 27 He answered and said, "You shall love the Lord your God with all your heart, and with all your soul, and with all your strength, and with all your mind; and your neighbor as yourself." 28 And he said to him, "You have answered correctly; do this, and you will live." 29 But wanting to justify himself, he said to Jesus, "And *who* is my neighbor?"

30 Jesus replied and said, "A certain man was going down from Jerusalem to Jericho, and fell among thieves, who stripped him and beat him, and went away leaving him half dead.

31 Now by chance, a priest was going down that road; and when he saw him, he passed by on the other side. 32 So likewise, a Levite, when he came to the place and saw him, passed by on the other side. 33 But a certain Samaritan while traveling came near him; and when he saw him, he had compassion. 34 He went to him and bandaged his wounds, pouring olive oil and wine; and he placed him on his own animal, brought him to an inn, and took care of him. 35 The next day, he took out two denarii, gave them to the innkeeper, and said, 'Take care of him; and whatever more you spend, when I come back, I will repay you.' 36 Which of these three, do you think, was a neighbor to the man who fell among the thieves?" 37 He said, "The one who showed him mercy." Jesus said to him, "Go and do likewise."

—LUKE 10:25-37

I ALWAYS HATED THE Jews—and with good reason: they hated us.

೨

Would you want your honor to be smashed like a jar in a thousand pieces? Imagine your humiliation when you make a long pilgrimage to present an offering in Jerusalem only to be barred from the temple. How would you react when Jews dismiss the Pentateuch you faithfully read and deeply cherish as merely a partial and inferior scripture? Feel the sting of being rebuked by strangers who maintain that they are the "pure" and "true" and the "only" Israel, despite your devotion and love of the Lord since the time of Moses. Think what it would be like to be viewed as a foreigner—in your own land! Would you want to be told that who you are and how you worship is worthless?[1] If so, welcome to the community of Samaritans.

೨

These tensions started long before I was born. My father's father would tell me stories of our ancestors who managed to remain in Israel's capital after the great invasion centuries ago.[2] While many inhabitants of Samaria were force to leave their homes and go to the land between the great rivers, a few people managed to avoid deportation, mostly by pretending to be dead amidst the city's carnage. Despite the tragedy that fell over Samaria and its inhabitants, this remnant of survivors remained ever faithful to the Lord. They maintained Samaritan traditions by worshipping on Mount Gerizim, as my ancestors had since the time of Moses.

Yet the religious leaders in Jerusalem insisted that Yahweh lived with *them* on Mount Zion. Almost gleefully, they noted that Jerusalem was spared while Samaria had been destroyed, as further proof of the Lord's favor. But in time their sense of triumph evaporated like water in the desert.

1. The name "Samaritan" comes from *shamarim* in Hebrew, meaning "those who guard" or "those who watch over" (the Torah). Samaritans had their own religious traditions and their own Pentateuch, which emphasized the importance of Mount Gerizim (one of the highest mountains in the region of Samaria). Tensions between Samaritans and Jews were strong, each group considering itself the true Israel. For further discussion, see Purvis, "Samaritans," 911–14.

2. This background refers to the conquest of the Northern Kingdom of Israel (capital: Samaria) by the Assyrians in 721 BCE and the conquest of the Southern Kingdom of Judah (capital: Jerusalem) by the Babylonians in 587 BCE. Many of the conquered inhabitants were forced into exile in Mesopotamia. Reasons for the schism between Jews and Samaritans are not entirely clear because our ancient sources are both limited and biased. Some scholars think this schism took place later than these events, during the Persian period. See Purvis, "Samaritans," 913–14.

Invaders came for Jerusalem too, and its inhabitants also knew brutal defeat and were forced to journey to a distant land. Two generations after this great deportation, some of the children and children's children of the exiled Jews returned to rebuild the Jerusalem temple.[3]

Although they had been dismissed as inferior, leaders from Samaria went south to offer their assistance. These efforts to aid in rebuilding were spurned and our leaders were told that no Yahwists of Samaria were welcome at the Lord's temple![4] This superior attitude has endured for many generations and hostilities have only increased. Do not blame me for my hatred of Jews. I am only living out the legacy of my people. Do you not do the same?

⤚

And so I try to avoid these self-righteous Jews as much as I can. It is hard because I am a merchant, but not merely a peddler who sells figs or nuts in the market. Do not insult me by attributing such lowly status to my occupation. Rather, I am a true tradesman who travels long distances to purchase fine foods and expensive wares then brings them to other regions. This work may not sound difficult to you, but consider all the risk that is involved. I need to know the value of all kinds of items and take care not to pay even one denarius[5] too much. I use my own denarii to obtain the goods, with no assurance that my purchases will sell for a price that covers my costs and travel. Then I must carry my wares, with only the help of my donkey. Yet by far the most treacherous part of my work is the journey on the roads. There on the highways, especially in the hills where they can easily hide, bandits lie in wait around the bends at night, seeking to take all that I have. If I keep my life, I'm lucky.

Like nearly all travelers, I have encountered misfortune. During one of my journeys, from Gitta to Neopolis,[6] I sat under a tree for a rest. I fell asleep and woke up to the sting of a scorpion on my foot, which quickly swelled and left me in great pain. I had no choice but to hobble home because my donkey was loaded with the goods that I had acquired. The only inns are in the towns, and there were none in sight. My pace was slow and darkness was coming, but what could I do? The feeling of dread grew in my

3. See Ezra 6:7–15.

4. See 1 Esd 5:63–71.

5. A denarius (plural: denarii) was a Roman coin worth about one day's wage for a common laborer.

6. These towns in the Samaritan region were about 12 miles apart, with only one city (Samaria or Sebaste) in between.

stomach as the sun started to sink in the hills. It turned out that I had good reason to fear.

As I rounded a bend in the road, I was attacked by a group of men. I always travel with a knife and immediately whipped it out to defend myself. Had I been without a weapon, I might have been killed. As it was, I lost all of my goods. The robbers left me only my donkey. They had no need of it (too slow), and ran off with what they had stolen from me.

Perhaps this is why I took pity, months later, on the heap of a man whom I encountered on another journey. This particular day I was going from Jerusalem to Jericho[7] with goods of exceptional quality: first press olive oil from the Mount of Olives, fresh red wine, and a long strip of smooth, white linen. These goods were far better than any made in Jericho and I knew that they would fetch a very high price. Although I had become more wary about making these trading trips after having been robbed, this route was much traveled by religious people of Jerusalem and therefore relatively safe. Furthermore, it was broad daylight, and I saw some other travelers on the road during that day, making my encounter with this particular stranger all the more surprising.

I was walking along the path about halfway between Jerusalem and Jericho when I heard a strange sound. No doubt other travelers had heard it too. Perhaps they thought the moan came from a dying animal? Perhaps they merely glanced in the direction of the curious noise from the bushes by the side of the road and moved on. Perhaps these travelers who kept walking were thinking about their own responsibilities, and knew (without thinking it) that to investigate the source of this moaning would be to take on trouble.

As with them, my first instinct was to keep going. Do not judge me. How many times have you done the same thing and walked past someone who was clearly a needy mess? And, truth be told, I also walked past these bushes at first. But the pitiful voice, and the realization that this wretched man could have been me—indeed, once was—made me stop, turn around, and find this pile of a person.

I have witnessed a lot in my travels, but I was not prepared for this sight. Whoever robbed this man had also felt compelled to beat him savagely. His body was bruised all over; blood was caked on his face and matted his hair. Flies were swarming around his head. How long had he been there? Many hours, at least, or more likely, since the night before.

---

7. The distance between Jerusalem and Jericho was about 15 miles, along a well-traveled route that wound through hills. See map in Curtis, *Atlas*, 146.

He could barely open his eyes, but I could sense his desperation. Mustering his remaining strength, he opened his eyes to look at me, and in that moment I knew that I could not leave him. Without thinking, I took a wine vessel off of my donkey and poured some of the precious red liquid into his mouth. He tried to drink, but his throat was nearly swollen shut. I then poured some wine on his wounds to clean them, followed by oil to soothe them, and wrapped the worst wounds with the linen. As I concentrated on my work, I sensed that this man was trying to say something to me, despite his battered state. When he managed to utter two syllables, I realized what I had done. "*Toda*," he barely whispered, his accent revealing him as a Jew. I had not spoken to him, just moved to clean his wounds. If I had uttered any words, would he still have said thank you, even though I am a Samaritan? For some reason, I didn't care.

I put the man on my donkey and led him to Anathoth.[8] I knew the innkeeper there, Chamis, from my travels. He was a kind man who would nurse this beaten Jew back to health. I had to stay the night as well since it was now dark, so I slept on a mat near this man, whose breath seemed to relax during the night. A few times I woke from my sleep to give him some water, which he managed to drink in small sips. When morning came, I gave Chamis two denarii and asked him to show this man the same hospitality I had received in the past. To have a generous reputation brings honor, so I added that I would pay Chamis the rest that he spent on this man's care upon my return.[9] However, I was quite sure that two denarii would be more than enough; the extra offer was to increase my honor. I was not planning to spend more on this Jew, already having given Chamis a good percentage of the profit that I had made in Jerusalem. However, I knew Chamis would tell others who stayed at the inn about my noble deed. Later, however, I realized that this might include fellow Samaritans. What if my people found out that I had helped a Jew? This worry consumed me for the next few days.

Yet as the days wore into weeks, I began to notice that my own views toward Jews had softened. My thoughts often wandered back to this beaten man and his whispered word of thanks. I found myself looking forward to

8. Anathoth lies between Jerusalem and Jericho, about 5 miles northeast of Jerusalem and 10 miles southwest of Jericho.

9. Honor was a foundational value and an organizing principle in ancient Mediterranean society. In the culture of Jesus' day, "A good honor rating is crucially necessary for a meaningful human social existence, much as a good credit rating is in our society." Malina, *Windows on the World of Jesus*, 1.

my next trip along this road so I could stop in Anathoth and ask Chamis what had happened to this stranger. I thought of him more as a man than a Jew. That surprised me.

On the day that my travels took me back to Chamis's inn, I tried not to sound overly curious.

"What happened to the Jew?" I asked casually.

"Ezer, you acted so kindly. You saved his life!" Chamis exclaimed, slapping me on the shoulder. "You cleaned him up well, and I continued to make sure his wounds were washed. With rest and good food, he slowly started to gain his strength back. Word spread quickly about his severe beating, and your generosity. After a few days, his brother came and took him home."

I found it hard to suppress a smile. Just as I had hoped, my honor had increased, albeit from another's misfortune.

"Did you get the man's name, Chamis?" I thought about trying to find him on my next trip to Jericho.

"He still did not remember his name during his time with me. When his brother came and took him, I was at the market. I do not know, Ezer."

Chamis then continued telling me the news of the area, as he always did.

"Ezer, there is a prophet in this area. I think you would be interested in him."

"Why?" I asked. Lots of people claim divine authority. Charlatans pay imposters to pretend they're sick then claim they were healed, gaining customers who give up large sums to the "prophet" to be "healed." "Is this the only news you have for me? That there is a prophet nearby?" I was unimpressed.

"This prophet *truly* heals," Chamis insisted. I remained skeptical as he continued, "Perhaps you could find him and bring him to cure that man's wounds."

Chamis was overestimating my concern for the Jew, but I had heard talk about a prophet unlike the others who actually did heal people.

Chamis continued, "This prophet would not let his disciples hurt Samaritans."[10] Now I was intrigued. "He went with his disciples down the road. Perhaps you can find them."

I was headed down that road anyway, but I will admit that my heart skipped a beat when I found myself nearing this prophet and his followers. It was not a large band, maybe ten people or so, at first. I could tell that the man in front was the prophet by the way the others looked at him, with

---

10. See Luke 9:51–56.

reverence and awe, as they walked alongside him. People came out of their homes to see him; some even joined the group. This prophet clearly had a strong reputation and people wanted whatever he had. I quickened my pace until I too had become part of the moving cluster around this man with the magnetic personality. As long as I kept my mouth shut, I blended in easily with the others. I was curious to hear what people were saying to this mysterious man.

A young man, closer to a boy, ran in front of the prophet, then turned to him and proclaimed impetuously, "I will follow you wherever you go."[11]

This prophet (they called him Jesus) told the youth that to join his group of followers was an invitation to homelessness. "The foxes have dens, and birds of the sky have nests; but the Son of man has nowhere to rest his head."

Glancing at a person on the side of the road who seemed eager, but reluctant, to join the group, Jesus called, "Follow me."

The man's reason for his reservations became clear. "Lord, permit me to first go and bury my father."

Jesus kept moving and called as he passed the man, "Leave the dead to bury their own dead; but as for you, go and proclaim the kingdom of God." The man remained where he was, clearly confused. How could the dead bury themselves? He should abandon his sacred duty to his deceased father? Why? What did it mean to "proclaim the kingdom of God"?

Then someone else near him got up and pleaded, "I will follow you Lord, but first allow me to say farewell to those at my home." Surely this prophet must respect the need to honor one's *living* family.

But the prophet remained steadfast; either you were fully committed to his mission or you were not welcome. "No one, after putting his hand to the plow and looking back, is fit for the kingdom of God." He kept walking.

Even on the edge of this traveling crowd, I could sense that this prophet was different. People wanted to be near him, even as he dismissed them. Perhaps his allure was *because* he dismissed them? He seemed intent on his work, something having to do with a kingdom. His stride was purposeful; he was deeply confident but also caring. Charisma attracts followers, and I found that I too was drawn to him.

I did not know if I would ever see this prophet again, so I made my way through the crowd. By picking up my pace and jostling purposefully, I got right next to him.

---

11. See Luke 9:57–62.

"Prophet, may I ask you a question?" As soon as the words came out of my mouth, I realized that he would know where I was from. I worried for a moment what he would think of me, but this man looked right at me and smiled.

"Certainly, faithful Samaritan." I felt relieved; he did not hate me.

I continued, "What will happen to someone who helps another, not of his own people? If his people find out, will they turn on him as they feel that he has turned on them?" I could not shake the worry that my fellow Samaritans would find out that the man I had helped was a Jew and view me harshly. I had wanted to increase my honor, but what if I had jeopardized it instead, thereby hurting my business?

"Tell me more," the prophet said, his pace slowing. He was nearly oblivious to those around him. He stopped and faced me, giving me his full attention. "A good teacher is a good listener; one must listen to serve."

As the prophet stopped, people sat down to take a break, clustering in small groups, talking among themselves. Some pulled out bundles of food and started to eat, freely sharing with one another. Jesus sat down next to me, both of us by the side of the road, and I told him what had happened.

"I am a merchant. One day while traveling, I helped a Jew. He had been beaten by robbers so I took him and brought him to an inn. Eventually he got better, but I worry that my kinsmen will think that I betrayed them by helping a Jew."

Why did I feel so comfortable talking to him? Why was I telling him this story? Maybe I wanted him to tell it to others? But by increasing my honor, was I also endangering my standing with my own people? I was confused and hoped that this man might help me understand the actions that had consumed so much of my thinking.

Jesus paused for a moment, considering what I had said.

"Then why did you do it?" he asked.

"Because it needed doing," I replied without thinking. As I said this, I realized that these words were true.

He looked straight into my eyes. "Truly I tell you, those who would disregard a Jew in need will answer to God upon their arrival at the Shepherd's Gate."

"But is your God just the God of the Jews? What about Gentiles and Samaritans?" I asked. Did the teachings of this prophet even apply to me, as a Samaritan?

"My God is our Father in Heaven. If you want to see the kingdom of God, you will follow the way and love God and your neighbor," said Jesus. With that, he got up and resumed walking, as did the others.

But not me. I waited until the crowd had moved on before I continued down the road. I needed to think about what this prophet had said, and hopefully understand it. What did it mean to "see the kingdom" and "follow the way"? What "way" was he talking about? Was he instructing me to obey the Torah of the Jews? How does one love God and one's neighbor? Was I ready to love *all* my neighbors, including the Jews? I doubted it.

↜

As my life resumed its usual routine, I had hoped that the memories of my encounter with the prophet would fade, yet this was not to be. More and more people were talking about Jesus as stories of his miracles spread. Fantastic rumors swirled that he even could make food multiply! I remained suspicious of that claim, but one could not deny that large crowds were seeking him out, pleading for healing, begging for him to remove demons, devouring his words. Now, just a few months after my conversation with the prophet, a person could not get next to him as easily as I had. Some people were getting nervous that he was garnering too much attention, and thought it was dangerous to be seen with him. But he kept on attracting followers because of his sense of purpose, and his compassion. People I knew from Samaria told stories of his kindness.[12]

I decided that I would go hear this prophet the next time I encountered him, which turned out to be a few weeks later when I was in Jericho. One afternoon while I was in the market gathering my goods, people started rushing past me toward the open square.

"The prophet—he's here!"

"Come, see him!"

"It's the Son of God!"

This was the kind of reputation that this prophet now enjoyed.

I followed the crowd to the square, and there he was, standing on some steps, preaching to a spellbound crowd. Most people seemed enraptured by his message, but there were a few skeptics who sat on the sidelines, their arms crossed, slight scowls on their faces. At one point, Jesus turned and said something to his inner circle of followers, most of whom I recognized

12. See Luke 17:11–19; John 4:4–42.

from that day on the road.[13] One of the skeptics overheard something he said, and got to his feet. The crowd hushed, worried that the encounter would be tense. The man's tunic of fine linen and his air of power gave him instant respect. He spoke as a learned man with authority.

"Teacher," he said, a touch of irony in his voice, "What shall I do to gain eternal life?"

Jesus smiled calmly. "What is written in the law? What do you read?" He was giving this man a chance to increase his honor by showing his knowledge to the crowd.

The man smirked at his companions because the answer was obvious. He confidently quoted the Torah: "You shall love the Lord your God with all your heart, and with all your soul, and with all your strength and with all your mind; and your neighbor as yourself."

Jesus nodded. "You have answered correctly; do this, and you will live."

This powerful man was not done, however. He needed to test Jesus further. In a condescending tone he asked, "And *who* is my neighbor?"

What happened next stunned me. Out of everyone in that square, perhaps as many as two hundred people, Jesus looked right at me as I stood at the far edge of the crowd. How had he seen me? How did he know I was there? Time slowed. I would not have believed that he was looking at me, but other heads turned in my direction to stare, until he began to speak.

Jesus then told this story:

"A certain man was going down from Jerusalem to Jericho, and fell among thieves, who stripped him and beat him, and went away leaving him half dead. Now by chance, a priest was going down that road; and when he saw him, he passed by on the other side. So likewise, a Levite, when he came to the place and saw him, passed by on the other side. But a certain Samaritan while traveling came near him; and when he saw him, he had compassion. He went to him and bandaged his wounds, pouring olive oil and wine; and he placed him on his own animal, brought him to an inn, and took care of him. The next day, he took out two denarii, gave them to the innkeeper, and said, 'Take care of him; and whatever more you spend, when I come back, I will repay you.'"

Fortunately, all eyes were on Jesus as he spoke because I had turned white with shock. Although I had told the prophet this story, he told much to the crowd that I had not revealed to him. I had not told him about the cleaning the man's wounds or giving Chamis two denarii. Even if someone

13. See Luke 10:23–24.

else had told him those details, this prophet told parts of the story that *I* didn't know. No one did. Had a priest and a Levite passed this man first? It seemed plausible, even likely on a road from Jerusalem, but I had not seen this. The rest of the story was exactly correct, so I surmised that this part was as well. *How did he know?* In that moment, like never before, I understood that this prophet was very different from the others. I whispered to myself, "How could he *not* know?"

Jesus then turned his attention from the crowd to the lawyer and asked, "Which of these three, do you think, was a neighbor to the man who fell among the thieves?"

The cocky questioner had been moved by the prophet's story. His voice was softer now, even humble. He said quietly, "The one who showed him mercy."

Jesus replied simply, "Go and do likewise."

↜

I realized that this great prophet was honoring me, a Samaritan. He did not care about my selfish motives or questions; he cared about acts of compassion. This must be what he meant when he spoke about "the kingdom" and "the way."

More than healing the sick, more than casting out evil spirits, more than feeding many people, perhaps I had just witnessed this prophet's greatest miracle. He made everyone in that crowd, me included, confront our cherished hatreds. And he did it simply by showing me—a Samaritan—as good.

Discussion Questions

1. The Samaritan in this story is deeply prejudiced in his dislike of Jews, but still acts compassionately to someone in need. Can someone be prejudiced and still be a good person? If not, why not? If so, does this acceptance help us tolerate our prejudices?

2. In this story, the Samaritan who helps the man by the side of the road is aware that he is also helping himself and his reputation with this action. Are our acts of kindness toward others ever purely altruistic? Why or why not?

3. Jesus has a profound influence on the Samaritan, even though they have only a single one-on-one conversation. Think of a person you

know (not a relative) who has exerted significant influence on your life. Why did this person have such an impact? Is there any particular encounter that stands out in your mind?

Bibliography

Curtis, Adrian. *Oxford Bible Atlas*. 4th ed. New York: Oxford University Press, 2007.

Malina, Bruce J. *Windows on the World of Jesus: Time Travel to Ancient Judea*. Louisville: Westminster John Knox, 1993.

Purvis, James D. "Samaritans." In *HarperCollins Bible Dictionary*, edited by Mark Allan Powell, 911–14. 3rd ed. New York: HarperCollins, 2011.

Fisherman

KENYATTA HUGHES

1 After these things Jesus showed himself again to the disciples by the Sea of Tiberias; and he showed himself in this way. *2* There were together Simon Peter, Thomas called the Twin, and Nathanael from Cana in Galilee, the sons of Zebedee, and two others of his disciples. *3* Simon Peter said to them, "I am going fishing." They said to him, "We will go with you." They went out and got into the boat, but during that night they caught nothing.

4 As morning was coming, Jesus stood on the shore; however, the disciples did not know that it was Jesus. *5* Jesus said to them, "Children, you do not have any fish, do you?" They answered him, "No." *6* He said to them, "Cast the net on the right side of the boat, and you'll find some." So they cast it, and now they were not able to haul it in because of the quantity of fish! *7* Then that disciple whom Jesus loved said to Peter, "It's the Lord!" When Simon Peter heard that it was the Lord, he put on a garment, for he was naked, and threw himself into the sea. *8* But the other disciples came in the boat, for they were not far from the land (around two hundred cubits away), dragging the net of the fish.

9 Then as soon as they got out upon the land, they saw a charcoal fire set up, with fish on it, and bread. *10* Jesus said to them, "Bring some of the fish that you caught now." *11* So Simon Peter got up and dragged the net on the land, full of big fish, a hundred fifty-three of them; and though there were so many, the net was not ripped. *12* Jesus said to them, "Come, have breakfast." But none of the disciples dared to ask him,

"Who are you?" knowing that it was the Lord. *13* Jesus came and took the bread and gave it to them, and did likewise with the fish. *14* This was now the third time that Jesus revealed himself to the disciples after he was raised from the dead.

15 When they had finished breakfast, Jesus said to Simon Peter, "Simon son of John, do you love me more than these?" He said to him, "Yes, Lord; you know that I have deep love for you." Jesus said to him, "Feed my lambs." *16* A second time he said to him, "Simon son of John, do you love me?" He said to him, "Yes, Lord; you know that I have deep love for you." Jesus said to him, "Keep my sheep." *17* He said to him the third time, "Simon son of John, do you have deep love for me?" Peter was pained because he said to him the third time, "Do you love me?" And he said to him, "Lord, you perceive everything; you know that I have great love for you." Jesus said to him, "Feed my sheep. *18* Very truly, I tell you, when you were younger, you used to fasten your belt yourself and moved about wherever you wished. But when you grow old, you will stretch out your hands, and another will fasten a belt around you and bring you where you do not wish to go." *19* (He said this signifying the kind of death by which he would glorify God.) And after this he said to him, "Follow me."

20 Turning around, Peter saw the disciple whom Jesus loved following; the one who had leaned on his chest at the supper and had said, "Lord, who is the one who will betray you?" *21* When Peter saw him, he said to Jesus, "Lord, what about him?" *22* Jesus said to him, "If I desire him to stay until I come, what is that to you? You follow me!" *23* So the word went forth in the community that this disciple would not die. But Jesus did not say to him that he would not die, but, "If I desire him to stay until I come, what is that to you?"

24 This is the disciple who is witnessing concerning these things and has written them, and we know that his witness is true.

—*JOHN 21:1-24*

PETER WANTED TO GO fishing, which we often did together since we both worked the boats in Capernaum.[1] I had been seeing less of him recently so I agreed, even though it was too cold. Then some of the men with whom he had grown so close said that they would come as well: the Twin, Nathaniel, the Zebedee brothers James and John, and a couple others. I had heard rumors about this group, yet I did not say that they should probably not be all together. I did not want them to think that I was afraid.

Peter carried the net. Both John and James tried to take a turn, but he waved them off. I knew better than to ask if he wanted help. Peter had always been headstrong, and this had not changed since he joined this group. So many other things had. He was almost never home, and even his mother, who loved him and swore the man Peter followed was a healer, even she became nervous when Peter was around. He would never have been called gentle, but now he was confrontational, combative.

From the first time he met this rabbi he had been following, Peter was changed—from the *very first*. I remember when Andrew came running to where Peter and I sat mending nets. Peter was teasing me for complaining, saying that I had the soft hands of a publican.[2] Andrew came upon us, wild-eyed and breathless, claiming to have met the Messiah. Peter said nothing, just dropped his net and followed his brother back the way he had come.

I did not see him again until two weeks later, when his wife's mother, Mariam, fell ill. I had been sitting with Peter's wife and mother-in-law for most of the day, but I had to leave. It is not good to be at a man's house when he is not there, especially if his wife is lamenting that he is spending too much time elsewhere. When I returned in the evening, a crowd so great I could not get through was surrounding Peter's house. Some of the people were blind, some lame, some raving. It looked like a nightmare. While I stared in uncomfortable awe, Peter appeared beside me at the edge of the crowd.

"Come!" he said. "He is inside! He has healed Mariam, and many more![3] Come, meet him!"

---

1. Capernaum is a fishing village on the north side of the Galilee, well-known to Jesus and his disciples. See, for example, Matt 8:5; Mark 1:21; 2:1; Luke 4:23. According to Matt 4:13, Jesus made his home there.

2. "Publican" is another word for "tax collector" (used in the King James Version). Publicans were usually wealthy and oversaw collection of taxes, hiring underlings to gather goods and revenue. Powell, *Bible Dictionary*, 1012. They did not work with their hands, hence the reference above.

3. The account of Jesus healing Peter's mother-in-law appears in all three Synoptic Gospels, although she remains anonymous (see Matt 8:14–15; Mark 1:30–31; Luke 4:38–39).

He grabbed my hand and pulled me toward the house, into the throng of hurting people. The press made it too hard to move forward, and I lost hold of his hand. I slipped back out and hurried home.

A few weeks passed, and I had only seen Peter one time since that day. Horrible things had happened to the man that he followed; I thought that now things might quiet down. I had yet to explain to Peter how I'd felt, why I'd left his house. What he was saying, what they were claiming—it was dangerous, and they were speaking so openly. When the Pharisees came and asked me if I knew Peter, I told them no. I had hoped to speak to him now that we were about to go fishing, but the others had come with us to the sea and there was no chance to talk privately.

Later when we reached the lake, it was well into the night. No one else was on the shore, but I could see a couple of boats in the starlight a little way out into the water, the men and the vessels' shadows on the ink of the sea. We grabbed our boat and turned it right side up, James and I taking the prow, while Nathanael and the Twin grabbed the stern. John tossed the line into the boat, and then offered to help with carrying the net, but Peter waved him off. Peter hauled the net into the boat with a grunt, and then leaned against the boat's side. His breathing was ragged, almost as if he were crying. I wanted to say something, but I didn't know what.

Before I realized what was happening, Peter had shifted his grip on the side of the boat and started pushing it toward the water. The boat barely moved at all, but I was surprised because he didn't say anything, didn't even check to make sure everyone was ready. Nathanael and the Twin must have felt the shift first, and they started pushing from the rear, but James was caught unawares. He stumbled and cursed under his breath, but then everybody was together and whatever he said was drowned out by the sound of the hull scraping against the gravel of the beach. We pushed the boat to the water. It was cold on my legs.

Each of us gave a short yell as we swung into the boat, a little bark to say we were safely aboard. It was the first time I'd heard Peter speak since declaring that he was going fishing. I started opening the nets, even though Peter was acting so possessive. He joined me, working wordlessly at the roughly knotted netting. He tugged more violently than necessary, so much so that I thought even fingers as calloused as his must hurt. I said nothing, continuing to work as the others rowed the boat out to deeper water. Occasionally, a word or two spoken by the men in the other boats floated faintly from the dark, but we mostly heard just the sound of the waves lapping the hull.

When the nets and line were ready, I began to undress as James shook the net out for a cast. As I turned from putting my clothes in the rear of the boat, I noticed that Peter had removed his robe as well.

It has been long since he was in the water, I thought. *Perhaps this will be good for him.* Peter and I had not been close, but we had fished together, back before he joined this bunch. Since then, he had become so intense, openly speaking against the authorities, all but explicitly advocating revolution. And now, these last days, he and the others were saying that the Nazarene had come back after his crucifixion—not that he had escaped and returned, but that he had *died* and *come back.* It was crazy, and I wanted to tell him, but he was nearly as bad as the zealots, almost manic in his insistence. To be honest, I was a little bit afraid. There was something unsettling in how enthusiastically he proclaimed the coming demise of this age and advent of the next. Who in their right mind looks forward to the end of the world?

James threw the net, and I waited, knowing that Peter would want to dive first. He did, jumping into the water as soon as the net's weights could have touched down.[4] While we waited for him to come back up, I looked at the other men. Not speaking, they just kept looking to one another. Even in the darkness, I could see the expression on their faces, something like wonder mixed with confusion. I felt left out, the only one not part of the group.

It occurred to me that Peter had been under a little long. Turning to the water, I watched for his head to break the surface. The moments stretched and I began to worry. Could he be caught in the net? He was far too experienced for that, but he had been away from fishing—*real* fishing— for over three years. Look how soon after the cast he had dived in, almost

---

4. According to an article by James A. Patch in the *International Standard Bible En-cyclopedia*, net fishing in this period and region was generally done in one of three ways: (1) a weighted tight meshed circular net is cast from the shore into the shallow water, trapping fish unable to escape the fisher's throw; (2) a long net, with weights along one edge and floats on the other, is splayed out between two boats many yards apart, and ten to twenty men gradually draw in the net by long ropes fastened to the two ends; (3) in deeper water, a net similar to that just described, but larger, is cast from a boat and the ends are brought together to form a circle. Men then dive down and drag one part of the weighted edge under the rest, forming an enclosure. The net is then drawn into the boat and emptied, or the net, with the fish enclosed, is towed into shallow water before drawing. While the second method is most commonly practiced on the shore of the Sea of Galilee, Patch contends that the third method is probably the one the disciples used (Matt 4:18; Mark 1:16; Luke 5:2–10; John 21:3–11). Patch, "Fishing," http://www.internationalstandardbible.com/F/fishing.html.

chasing the net. Even a novice would know better than that. I looked at the others, but they were still lost in whatever thoughts come of having your rebellion crushed. They would be no help.

I was just about to tell them to draw in the net when I heard the splash and gasp of Peter breaking the water. He swam the short distance to the boat, his strokes sure and even. I felt a little embarrassed that I had been concerned, even if no one else knew. I reached down to clasp his hand when he reached the side, pulling him into the boat.

"Thanks," he said.

I did not respond, instead turning to help James and John bring in the net. It was a little awkward; the boat usually held six, maybe seven, and eight men was tight. It didn't matter, anyway, since the net came up with no effort at all, empty. James gathered it in, twisted at the middle, then whipped around to stand with his arms outstretched as he cast the net into the water. This time, I dove, admittedly, a little too soon. I was worried about Peter, and wanted to get in the water before he did.

The shock of the cold sea made me regret agreeing to come; it really wasn't the right time for this. There was no light beneath the waves, and no sound but that constant, dull roar that fills the ears underwater. I kicked down to the sea floor, feeling my way to where the bottom of the net lay. Grabbing the weighted edge, I dragged it over to the other end. After folding one edge over the other, I pushed off the bottom, kicking and stroking my way up. As I came up for air and started swimming toward the boat, I realized why Peter might have wanted to fish at a time like this. For the short while that I was under water, there were no rebels, no soldiers, no Sanhedrin, no messiah—dead or alive. There was nothing but the water, the net, and the breath I had left. When I got to the boat, it was Peter's hand that reached down to pull me up.

"Thanks," I said. He grunted in response.

We drew the net in again, and again it was empty. James cast several times, Peter and I taking turns in the water; every time, no fish. Eventually John made a joke, and James challenged him to try. John did, but he brought in the same thing that James had: empty nets.

At first, I did not mind. After the initial shock of the sea, the diving was quite soothing, and Peter and his friends seemed to grow more comfortable. But as the night wore on and there was no catch, I tired of the repetition. Clearly, there were no fish to be caught; every fisherman knows that happens sometimes. Peter should have known as well, but he just grew more determined. What little joking had begun disappeared, replaced by a growing tension and sense of urgency. There would be no fish, but I didn't want to be that one to cry off. They would give up eventually.

But they didn't. Instead, we continued for hours, still casting, as the black of night became the gray of dawn. Still alternating with Peter, I dove, the act having long since lost any enjoyment it originally gave. When I came back up, James was shouting to someone on the shore, apparently another fisherman.

"No!" he called, voice tinged with bitterness. "There is nothing to be had!"

Well, if you knew that, I thought as I swam to the boat, *why are we still out here, you ass?*

I climbed in, moving to the back of the boat as the Twin and John drew in the empty net. I picked up my robe; James, having said aloud what we all knew to be true, would finish this fruitless night, and we could go home. I heard the voice of the fisherman on the shore.

"Cast the net on the right side of the boat and you'll find some!"

If I were not already tired, his advice might have seemed like encouragement; instead, it was irritating. Even more irritating, I realized that John was actually preparing to do it.

This is ridiculous. Once we brought the net back in, I was leaving, with or without them. They had to realize how dangerous it was for them to still be about as daylight came. I had nothing to do with the things they were involved in, and had no desire to suffer for being in their company, especially since we weren't going to catch any fish. Peter dove into the water and was back up by the time I had put on my robe. Letting someone else help him in, I grabbed the net and began to draw it in, long past ready for this trip to end.

Immediately, I knew that something was wrong. The net was dragging far too heavily. In his haste, Peter must have snagged the weights on the bottom, or somehow fouled the nets. *Wonderful,* I thought, realizing this ordeal might be very far from over. I grabbed a fistful of net and pulled as hard as I could. It came, if too heavily, so at least it wasn't snagged. Nathanael was pulling as well, and I could tell that he knew something was wrong.

"John," he said, the strain clear in his voice, "help draw."

"Together," said John, joining us. "One . . . two . . . three!"

We leaned back as we pulled, groaning with the effort. I looked down at our hands clutching the net, at the muscles of John's forearms straining as the net began to come up. Slowly, I realized that the net wasn't coming to the boat. Instead, the boat was dragging to the net as we slowly moved closer to the shore. I could see down in to the water, and the net was full of fish, more than I'd seen in a haul, more than I thought was possible.

"What . . .?" I said.

"*Rabboni!*" John cried.

Turning to look at the figure, John released the net so suddenly that I almost fell in the water. Peter *did* go in, wrapping a garment around himself and swimming to the shore. My heart jumped within me, though I wasn't sure if John was right. I *was* sure that if someone did not help me, we would lose the fish *and* the net.

"We tried all night for fish," I said, trying to sound less frustrated than I felt. "It would be a shame to leave our only full net."

John returned to the net, and he, Nathanael, and I held it while the others rowed us in. Peter, now on the beach, ran over to us, helping as we jumped out of the boat and dragged the net up onto the shore. The early morning light reflected on the wriggling silver of what must have been well over a hundred fish, huge ones—the biggest I'd ever seen. I sat down on the ground, panting, staring at them. Peter immediately opened the net and grabbed several.

"The *rebbe* wants fish," he said, out of breath. His strong hands were full of writhing silver creatures. Peter turned and ran back to where the figure sat before a fire, facing away from me. Without turning to look at us, the mysterious man called out, "Come, have breakfast." Leaving the boat and the nets, the others ran behind Peter; I stood and walked after them.

Throughout these recent years, as Peter and his new friends had stirred up so much trouble, I had never actually seen this "messiah." The crowd at Peter's house was nothing compared to the mobs that later came to follow this prophet. There were always scores of people wanting healing, crying out for this "Son of David." If you wanted to get close enough to see the man they were calling for, you had to press through a thick ring of sick and disfigured people. There were even some among them who were unclean, wanting to be touched, and you could not make it to this messiah unless you were willing to come in contact with the unclean ones. I could never bring myself to do it.

If this were him, now, sitting on the beach, I would finally see him.

When I reached the fire, the man was already giving out fish and bread that he'd had on the coals. John took a portion and passed it back to me. I sat, not quite in the circle, and still unable to see the man's face. I ate hungrily and listened. He asked why they had been fishing, and James told him it had been Peter's idea. The man seemed to be teasing with the question, and James certainly seemed a little sheepish about answering it.

"Simon, son of John" the man said to Peter, and gestured toward the fish. "Do you love me more than these?"

"Yes, *rabboni*," Peter answered, somewhat surprised by the question. "You know that I have deep love for you."

"Feed my lambs," the man said.

I wondered what that meant, but the man offered no explanation. As I looked at his profile, he put a little morsel of bread in his mouth and began picking at a piece of fish. Unable to resist, I tried to see if there were wounds on his wrists, but his sleeves were too long.

"Simon, son of John," he said to Peter again, "do you love me?"

"Yes, *rabboni*—you *know* that I have deep love for you," Peter protested. There was pain in his voice, and I felt uncomfortable. The others must have felt it too, from the way they looked at one another. A spark of anger flared in my heart. How dare this man even ask that? If he had seen how distraught Peter was after hearing that the "King of the Jews" had been crucified . . . wasn't he supposed to be a prophet? Peter was at my house following the Passover, afraid to go to his own. I was there when John came slinking in the night, tapping at the door as if frightened of the sound that a true "knock" would make. The night after Jesus was killed, I heard John's halting, weeping whisper, and the long and raw cry that wrenched from Peter's throat. These were the sounds of men who cannot be comforted.

And now, having faked his death or . . . or *something*, he questioned Peter's love?

"Keep my sheep," the man told Peter. And then, before the sound of those had words had barely ended: "Simon, son of John, do you have *deep* love for me?"

"*Rabboni*," Peter said, near tears, "you perceive everything; you know that I have great love for you!"

I realized that Peter might start to cry, and wondered why this man would do this, in front of Peter's friends. Peter had given up everything to follow him; some of our old friends wouldn't even have him in their homes. If the Romans or the Sanhedrin found him—or any of the others—they would likely be executed. What more did this man want?

"Feed my sheep," the man told Peter, his voice little more than a whisper. "Very truly, I tell you, when you were younger, you used to fasten your belt yourself." He gestured as if putting on a garment, as Peter had just done leaving the boat, then added, "and moved about wherever you wished." With a twinkle in his eyes, he made a splashing sound and motioned his arms to imitate a quickly swimming Peter. "But when you grow old," the man said, the humor gone from his voice, "you will stretch out your hands, and another will fasten a belt around you and bring you where you do not wish to go." He reached over, laying his hand upon Peter's.

"Follow me," he said.

There was a prickle on the back of my neck; this was prophesying. Not the kind where they said something nebulous and open to interpretation, like the prophet in the marketplace with her "I see struggle followed by victory" or "two ways; but the end is unclear." She never said anything specific or unsettling. But this man was saying that Peter would be *arrested*, and maybe put in chains. If Peter did get arrested, whose fault would it be? The only thing he'd ever done wrong was join these rebels, and run around Palestine with people proclaiming this man king. And here I was, eating with them in the morning as the fishermen began to arrive, listening to this man predict that there were going to be arrests.

As I rose to leave, Peter turned.

"Lord," he asked the man, "what about him?"

My breath stopped in me, my entire body frozen; it felt almost exactly like last night's first plunge into the cold sea. I didn't know whether Peter was asking what they should do about me, or what the man foresaw for me. I could not have said at that moment which answer I feared more.

Then the man turned, and I realized Peter was talking about one of the other rebels, the youngest. It was my first chance to see the rabbi's face, but I was so relieved, I noticed little more than his expression of irritation as he turned back to Peter.

"If I desire him to stay until I come, what is that to you?" he said. "*You* follow me."

Peter said something in reply, but I didn't catch it; I was already moving away. Looking at them as I left, I saw what could only be called worship written on their faces. It made me nervous; I was going home. If Peter came to find me later, fine. If not, maybe better. To follow this man would cost everything, and every one of these men was willing to give it. I was not willing even to pay the cost of being seen with him.

As I passed the full net, a few of the fish still occasionally moving, it struck me as clear as prophecy that the Romans and Sanhedrin had no idea. They couldn't possibly realize all that they had started by ending one man's life. This group of Galileans was going to make more noise than ever, although those in power had thought that Jesus' rebel friends would be quiet with their leader gone . . .

Not so . . . Not so.

Discussion Questions

1. The narrator in "Fisherman" is a made-up character, but the ministry of Jesus and the witness of Peter are foundational to the Gospels. Do the portrayals of Peter and Jesus in this story accord with how you usually think of them? Why or why not?

2. Many Christians today imagine that they would have followed Jesus if they had lived in first century Palestine, but this essay highlights the very real dangers of being associated with him. Do you honestly think you would have followed Jesus? Why or why not?

3. The narrator of this story reasonably asks, "Who in their right mind looks forward to the end of the world?" However, both Jesus and the apostle Paul preach hopeful messages about the world's imminent destruction. Do you think they were "out of their minds"? Why or why not?

Bibliography

Patch, James A. "Fishing" in *International Standard Bible Encyclopedia*, edited by James Orr. Grand Rapids: Eerdmans, 1936. http://www.internationalstandardbible.com/F/fishing.html.

Powell, Mark Allan, ed. *The HarperCollins Bible Dictionary*. 3rd ed. New York: HarperCollins, 2011.